Real World ASP.NET Best Practices

FARHAN MUHAMMAD AND MATT MILNER

a!™

apress™

Real World ASP.NET Best Practices
Copyright © 2003 by Farhan Muhammad and Matt Milner

ISBN (pbk): 1-59059-100-3

Printed and bound in the United States of America 12345678910

Trademarked names may appear in this book. Rather than use a trademark symbol with every occurrence of a trademarked name, we use the names only in an editorial fashion and to the benefit of the trademark owner, with no intention of infringement of the trademark.

Technical Reviewer: Scott Stabbert

Editorial Directors: Dan Appleman, Gary Cornell, Simon Hayes, Martin Streicher, Karen Watterson, John Zukowski

Assistant Publisher: Grace Wong

Project Manager: Tracy Brown Collins

Development Editor: Ami Knox

Copy Editor: Kristen Imler

Compositor and Proofreader: Kinetic Publishing Services, LLC

Indexer: Lynn Armstrong

Cover Designer: Kurt Krames

Production Manager: Kari Brooks

Manufacturing Manager: Tom Debolski

Distributed to the book trade in the United States by Springer-Verlag New York, Inc., 175 Fifth Avenue, New York, NY, 10010 and outside the United States by Springer-Verlag GmbH & Co. KG, Tiergartenstr. 17, 69112 Heidelberg, Germany.

In the United States: phone 1-800-SPRINGER, email orders@springer-ny.com, or visit http://www.springer-ny.com. Outside the United States: fax +49 6221 345229, email orders@springer.de, or visit http://www.springer.de.

For information on translations, please contact Apress directly at 2560 Ninth Street, Suite 219, Berkeley, CA 94710. Phone 510-549-5930, fax 510-549-5939, email info@apress.com, or visit http://www.apress.com.

The information in this book is distributed on an "as is" basis, without warranty. Although every precaution has been taken in the preparation of this work, neither the author(s) nor Apress shall have any liability to any person or entity with respect to any loss or damage caused or alleged to be caused directly or indirectly by the information contained in this work.

The source code for this book is available to readers at http://www.apress.com in the Downloads section.

I would like to dedicate this book to my lovely wife, Luna, whose continuous support and encouragement made this book possible. I would also like to dedicate this book to my parents, who taught me to do my best in everything I start.

—Farhan Muhammad

I would like to dedicate this book to my wife, Kristen, for the patience she exhibits about the many hours spent in front of the computer and the unlimited amount of support she provides for all my endeavors. I would not be where I am without her.

—Matt Milner

Contents at a Glance

Contents

About the Authors

FARHAN MUHAMMAD is the Chief Architect at ILM Professional Services. He is a technology enthusiast and has been an evangelist for the .NET technology since its inception. He leads the Twin Cities .NET User Group, a 400-member-strong community that focuses on sharing .NET knowledge among its members. He sits on the board of directors for the International .NET Association (INETA), where he is responsible for developing strategies for supporting .NET-focused communities in every corner of the world. He also leads INETA's Speakers Bureau, a very successful program that connects user groups throughout the U.S. with top-notch .NET experts. Farhan hosts the Executive .NET seminar on a regular basis, where executives are educated on the short- and long-term impact of the .NET technology on their businesses. He has a masters degree in software engineering from the University of Minnesota.

MATT MILNER is a consultant in Minneapolis, where he designs and develops .NET applications. He focuses on solving business problems by using Microsoft technologies and is enthusiastic about .NET's capabilities for building enterprise class applications. In addition to his work with clients, Matt enjoys helping others learn about .NET, which is why he has contributed to several other books and articles on .NET, and is an active participant and presenter in the local .NET user group.

About the Technical Reviewer

SCOTT STABBERT is a Program Manager at Microsoft. He has been a lead for the ASP developer support teams, written and conducted training for ASP.NET and Web services for Microsoft around the world, and is currently a technical resource for partners that are implementing Microsoft's .NET Passport and MSN Alerts services. Scott is a native of Redmond, WA, and used to launch rockets in the big empty field where Microsoft now sits.

Introduction

WE HAVE BEEN USING the ASP.NET framework actively since its early infancy (more than a year before official release) to program business solutions for corporate America. Just like most people, we started by purchasing a bunch of books and tried to use them to absorb as much knowledge as we possibly could. It didn't take too long for us to realize that none of those books gave us what we really needed. What we really needed was wisdom (not knowledge) on how to use the framework properly—what to do, what not to do, why things are the way they are, and why ASP.NET is not the best thing since sliced bread.

Knowledge is overrated. It can even be a plague, the kind that can eat your skills from the inside. A wise man once said, don't give me the knowledge of a hundred tools to do ten things; instead, show me ten ways to do a hundred things better.

The point we are trying to make is this: It is of higher importance for all of us to learn to use our tools appropriately, by leveraging other people's wisdom. The depth of the knowledge will come in time. What we all need currently is to focus on not making rookie mistakes. There is no shame in failure. We are not against failure. In fact, we acquire most of our wisdom by making mistakes and later rectifying those mistakes. However, while we work for other individuals or corporations, it is our responsibility to make fewer mistakes by learning from other people's experiences.

This book is also full of our opinions. We figured that if you spend your money buying our book, you deserve to know what we really think. Feel free to disagree with us and even let us know why you do.

This book shows best practices and some cautions related to various areas of the ASP.NET framework. We start this book by admiring the code-behind programming model, arguably one of the best features that ASP.NET provides. We are in love with the code-behind style of Web programming. In fact, it was this particular feature that initially attracted both of us toward exploring the rest of ASP.NET framework.

After admiring the code-behind style of programming, we move on to Chapter 2, where we discuss ways to store data in memory so that we can provide much-needed relief to the database servers. In particular, we spend much time discussing various caching mechanisms and conduct a series of performance tests to discuss best practices. After discussing caching mechanisms, we start on best practices related to session management. A good discussion on caching wouldn't be complete without delving into a discussion on view state, and we close this chapter by showing various issues related to view state and how to best use it to our advantage.

One of our pet peeves with .NET is its support of client side JavaScript, or lack thereof. We dedicated all of Chapter 3 to discussing JavaScript while showing best practices, as well as a healthy dose of cautions.

A best practices book wouldn't be complete without a discussion on data management, so in Chapter 4, we show best practices related to using ADO.NET. We have found many novice .NET programmers using the DataSet object extensively and felt that we should educate our readers on other, more advanced mechanisms. Though the DataSet object provides many useful features, it also comes with a price. Such shortfalls encouraged us to use this chapter to compare and contrast the DataSet object with other mechanisms.

We feel that we were extremely lucky to be consultants during the early days of ASP.NET technology. It gave us opportunities to work closely with many early adopters and learn about the common mistakes most novice programmers made. One such mistake was using the DataGrid Web server control for all list management needs. As with the DataSet object, we feel that the DataGrid control is overused. Sure, it is simple and easy to use and can be configured visually, but as a much heavier control, it causes many performance and scalability problems. We don't discourage you from using this control, but we wanted to dedicate Chapter 5 to discussing list management best practices.

Programmers often ask us about the difference between user controls and server controls. It can be difficult to determine which mechanism to use while developing reusable Web controls for your projects. The ASP.NET framework can sometimes be a little ambiguous; it provides multiple ways in which to accomplish the same purpose with subtle differences in each way. We dedicated Chapter 6 to discussing the difference between these two ways of creating Web controls and showing you the best practices related to each mechanism.

Not a month goes by when we don't see at least one example of novice .NET programmers using Web services for distributed programming when remoting would be a better alternative. We felt that the sheer volume of such clear misuse of Web services warranted a chapter of its own. Hence, Chapter 7 focuses entirely on comparing the differences between remoting and Web services and showing best practices for each approach.

ASP.NET introduces an innovative mechanism to configure Web applications: the web.config file. Chapter 8 focuses on educating readers on best practices for using the web.config file, including creating custom XML-based configuration sections.

ASP.NET is a wonderful new enabling technology that allows us to create business solutions much more effectively than ever before. However, there is much room for improvement. You won't often see the potholes and pitfalls related to these technologies simply by reading the books. Instead, you must experience them by shedding sweat and blood. (Okay, not blood!) We hope this book helps you, the reader, avoid such roadblocks and find easier ways as you become accustomed to ASP.NET.

CHAPTER 1

The Age of ASP.NET

IT WAS THE BEST OF TIMES, it was the worst of times. It was the age of creativity, it was the age of complexity, it was the era of accomplishments, it was the chronometry of failed dreams. All in all, ASP and VBScript were the two technologies that made Web applications possible for so many of us and, in return, demanded our sweat, blood, frustration, patience, and, most important of all, our loyalty.

Things shall never be the same again. With the introduction of ASP.NET, we are no longer bound by the limitations of these two technologies. We now have choices! We can choose to use virtually any programming language we want. We can choose to declare variables of specific types. We can choose to early bind to our objects, if we want. Most important of all, we can separate our code from presentation elements.

These are wonderful times. We, the programmers, are now free to code to our liking. However, with freedom comes responsibility. We have the responsibility to use these new technologies to their fullest extent. We have the responsibility to learn from others' mistakes and to try not to make the same pitfalls.

In this chapter, we introduce ASP.NET concepts and share our experiences with programming Web applications that use ASP.NET.

The Concept of Code Behind: Separating Fact from Fiction

Code behind, an innovative concept introduced in ASP.NET, allows us to separate programming logic completely from presentation elements. Until the introduction of the code-behind style of programming, a typical Web page consisted of a template HTML file riddled with inline programming code to support dynamic content and interactive behavior. While this technique proved useful in the early days of Web application development, it also proved very difficult to manage, debug, and reuse. The problems related to inline programming code will multiply as Web applications become increasingly interactive and complex.

Code behind is a new concept for many developers of traditional ASP and VBScript technologies. These programmers, however, have used a concept similar to code behind when working with business logic by encapsulating it into a COM component. It is still a common practice among developers of traditional ASP and VBScript programs to intersperse lots of implementation code in the .asp file, constantly switching between HTML and VBScript. While developers can break out some code from the HTML by using include files for improved reusability, it is really impossible to separate the two cleanly.

BEST PRACTICE *A code-behind file is not meant to provide a container for business logic code. It is simply a place for writing user-interface management code. Consider a code-behind file analogous to the code window used in Windows applications. A Windows application provides a code window for each form, which is meant for placing code used for managing the user interface; it is not a place for putting business logic code. The code-behind file essentially serves the same purpose: It should hold only user interface implementation code and serve as the first tier in a three-tier programming model. Business and data-access logic should be written in their own class libraries, as they represent the second and third tiers. The first tier is broken into two pieces: user interface elements and user interface implementation. The user interface elements are contained in the .aspx file, whereas the user interface implementation is contained in the code-behind file.*

The ASP.NET programming model provides us with the flexibility to remove all program code from the presentation elements and place them separately in another file. This separation of program code from presentation elements allows the graphics design team to focus on their tasks without interfering much with the programmers. It solves many common sources of complaints among programmers, graphics designers, and even project managers.

We have seen it too many times, as we are sure most of you have. The graphics team creates the original work of art, and the programmers take it and rip it apart by removing vital HTML elements and replacing them with some weird (really awful) VBScript syntax. After the programmers convert the HTML pages to ASP pages, it becomes virtually impossible for the graphics designers to maintain and update the content. Project managers, on the other hand, are constantly challenged to balance team resources by keeping programmers busy writing program code, not updating graphical elements.

A Dream Come True!

I had a dream, a wonderful dream. It was a dream that until two years ago seemed impossible. I still remember that lonely night when I worked late into the evening trying to apply last-minute design changes to a newly developed Web application. It wasn't that I didn't enjoy getting messy with raw HTML, but I had a lot of programming assignments with tight deadlines. Our graphics designers had gone home early; they hadn't had much to do. Though they had created these Web pages, they had failed to maintain them effectively after we significantly butchered their HTML while trying to convert them into ASP pages. It wasn't that the graphic designers were scared of angel brackets (<% %>), but the sheer complexity of dozens of lines of HTML and hundreds of lines of VBScript made it too risky for them to make design changes. The problem became even more complicated by our use of multiple nested include files.

That night when I got home close to midnight, I had this dream. My work was still incomplete, with no sign of completion in the near future. I dreamed about a workplace where graphics designers worked together with programmers throughout the project life cycle. Both were able to check out their respective files from the source control and work on them independently, without affecting each other's work. In my dream, I saw clearly that HTML had no program code embedded in it. I also saw that the program code had no graphical elements embedded in it. It was the world of perfect harmony. I thought about that dream a lot. I thought about that dream all the time.

It has been close to two years since I first started programming with ASP.NET. From the time I first laid my eyes on it, I knew that my dream would come true. I fell in love with its way of separating code from content. I couldn't wait to show it to my team members, graphics designers, project managers, and others. However, it wasn't until recently when Visual Studio .NET was released as a production version that I could convince people to take chances with this tool. I am happy to announce that we are in the process of teaching our graphics team the ways of ASP.NET. They are eager to learn server controls and to start using them to create and maintain .aspx pages. They will finally have the freedom they wanted. They will own all the .aspx pages in our project.

They will not only create them but will also maintain these pages. In the near future, when someone wants a new look and feel, the task will be assigned to the graphics designer and not to the developer. In the near future, if someone wants to update static content on the Web pages, the tasks will be assigned to the graphics designer and not to the developer. Oh, what a wonderful world that would be!

—Farhan Muhammad

The concept of code behind touches us in many ways. It is more than just another way of grouping program code; it is a new way of developing, maintaining, and managing Web applications.

The only issue we have encountered with assigning different individuals to work on .aspx and code behind files is Visual Studio .NET's desire to check out both files simultaneously. Visual Studio .NET attempts to update the code-behind file with the changes that are made to the .aspx file. For instance, renaming a server control by using the property window causes Visual Studio .NET to update the code behind file automatically to reflect the change. As a result, only one person can check out the Web page at a time, and the other person has to wait until the file is checked in.

The code-behind file treats the Web page as an object-oriented class. All controls contained in the page are members of the page class. We can control the behavior of the server controls by accessing their properties and methods in code behind. This programming model allows us to work with the controls independently of their visual elements and the visual elements of the page that contains them.

It can sometimes be tricky to distinguish between the responsibility of the code behind and that of the .aspx file. Consider, for example, a scenario in which you need to show a few lines of content on the page only if a certain condition is met. The obvious answer would be to declare a label control and to populate its content from the code behind if the condition is met.

```
if (some condition ...)
 {
    MyLabel.Text = "I need to show this text now";
 }
```

The problem occurs when you finish your project and deploy it to production and your users, predictably, change their minds and want to show different text. If you've worked in this field long enough, you probably expect this scenario. In your users' opinion, this simple change should require no time at all. After all, they are only asking for a change to static content, not to the programming logic.

Trust us, it has happened to us before. We once spent several months building a very large Web application with ASP.NET. After three weeks of intense testing, we were given the green light to start production deployment. Right when we were preparing to start the build and deployment procedure, we got a call from one of the business decision-makers asking us to change the grammar on one warning message on a specific Web page. We thought it to be a simple content change and agreed to make the change before deploying to production. Little did we know that the programmer had used code behind to populate the content on an empty label control!

At first we were reluctant to change the code moments before deploying to production, but we were assured by the programmer that making the change wouldn't introduce a new defect in the system. We're always skeptical of making code changes at the last moment and decided to redeploy the code to QA and ask them to test that page. This process caused us to miss our production window because we could update the production servers only during certain hours of low traffic. It wasn't fun when we had to explain to all the stakeholders next morning why we needed to wait a full day just to incorporate a very simple content change.

 BEST PRACTICE *We recommend that you keep all content in the .aspx file. If you need to show certain text based on a certain condition, you can always make the label controls visible or invisible as needed.*

Try to avoid making code changes to accommodate change in the content. It is not uncommon for a Web application to go through many more content changes than programming logic changes, especially after it is released to production and goes in the maintenance mode.

Some would argue that a better way for handling such tasks is by using a resource file, which would also help with localization. Our opinion on resource files is that they should be used if the system is being designed for use outside North America either currently or in future versions. Changing the content of a resource file also requires us to rebuild the project and redeploy the executable code, which is riskier than simply changing static content on an .aspx page and redeploying that one page alone. Yes, we can use satellite assemblies to isolate the content of resource files from other binaries, but it seems like too much work for systems that aren't intended for use outside North America and therefore don't require localization.

Another very useful feature that ASP.NET provides is the ability to inherit a code-behind file from a custom-built class. This feature helps us implement commonly used functionality across all Web pages in a consistent manner with a maximum amount of code reuse.

Using Inheritance in Code Behind

The code-behind model enables an incredibly powerful and often overlooked object-oriented programming technique in ASP.NET: inheritance, with which most programmers are at least conceptually familiar. Inheritance is the ability to create a base class that has some functionality that you want to reuse. Other classes then inherit from this base class and share some common implementation code.

The code-behind class must inherit from the System.Web.UI.Page class, but it doesn't have to inherit from it directly! A power technique involves creating a common base class for all or some subset of pages in your application. This base class inherits from the Page class, and your code-behind page would then inherit from this common base class, instead of directly from the Page class.

By using this method, you can create a power class to which you can add code that will instantly enable new functionality in any page you inherit from it.

In the following example, we create a base class that handles getting information in and out of session. It encapsulates the code for handling a situation when the session is empty. It is often a good idea to create a base class for some or all of your Web pages. You can use this base class to provide common functionality.

Listing 1-1 shows an example of a base Page class that can serve as a parent class for any number of ASP.NET Web pages.

Listing 1-1. An Example of a Base Page Class

```
' The enumeration is used to prevent hard-coded session key names.
' It is not a good practice to hard-code key names because it
' relies on programmers' memory to remember exact key syntax and
' may introduce defects in your system if the key name
' is used with incorrect spelling.
Public Enum SessionEnum
     UserID
     DateOfBirth
End Enum


' The base page class inherits from System.Web.UI.Page class.
Public Class PageBase
Inherits System.Web.UI.Page


' This delegate is used when the session is found empty.
' The method implementing this delegate will be responsible
' for retrieving information to be stored in session.
Delegate Function SessionEmptyDelegate() As Object


     ' Constructor
     Public Sub New()
     End Sub


' This method retrieves an object from session with matching
' key name.
     Public Function GetFromSession(ByVal keyName As SessionEnum, _
ByVal emptyCallBack As SessionEmptyDelegate)  As Object
     Dim ReturnObject As Object
```

```vb
    ' If session is empty, use CallBack to get its value.
    If Session(keyName.ToString()) = Nothing Then
        ReturnObject = emptyCallBack()
        PutInSession(keyName, ReturnObject)
    Else
        ReturnObject = Session(keyName.ToString())
    End If


    Return ReturnObject
End Function


' Putting an object in the session with specified key name.
    Public Sub PutInSession(ByVal keyName As SessionEnum, ByVal target As Object)
        Session(keyName.ToString()) = target
    End Sub
End Class


' The code behind class inherits from PageBase class. Because the base
' class inherits from System.Web.UI.Page class, this code behind class
' becomes a Web form.
Public Class Codebehind_Inheritance
    Inherits PageBase


' This page contains two buttons and a label control.
    Protected WithEvents PutButton As System.Web.UI.WebControls.Button
    Protected WithEvents GetButton As System.Web.UI.WebControls.Button
    Protected WithEvents ResultLabel As System.Web.UI.WebControls.Label


Private Sub Page_Load(ByVal sender As System.Object, _
                                    ByVal e As System.EventArgs) Handles
MyBase.Load
    End Sub


    ' Adding an object in the session by calling base class's
    ' PutInSession method.
Private Sub PutButton_Click(ByVal sender As System.Object, _
        ByVal As System.EventArgs) Handles PutButton.Click
        Me.PutInSession(SessionEnum.UserID, "Farhan")
    End Sub


    ' This method implements SessionEmptyDelegate defined in the
    ' base class.
    Private Function GetUserID() As Object
        Return "Farhan"
    End Function
```

```
' This method retrieves an object from session by calling base
' class's GetFromSession method. It also creates an object of
' SessionEmptyDelegate, which is used to call GetUserID method
' if the session is found empty.
    Private Sub GetButton_Click(ByVal sender As System.Object, _
                            ByVal e As System.EventArgs) Handles GetButton.Click

        Dim NoUserIDCallback As SessionEmptyDelegate
        NoUserIDCallback = New SessionEmptyDelegate(AddressOf GetUserID)

        ' Using CType method to convert returned generic object
        ' back to the String object.
        ResultLabel.Text = CType(Me.GetFromSession(SessionEnum.UserID, _
                            NoUserIDCallback), String)


    End Sub
End Class
```

An important part of separating the .aspx page from the code behind is somehow to connect events in the user interface to the appropriate method in the code behind that should serve as the event handler for that particular event. Connecting events sent to the .aspx page to their respective event handlers is referred to as *wiring* the event.

Event Wiring

Wiring an event handler to various events exposed by server controls is a significant part of the ASP.NET Web form. You can wire an event handler to an event in several ways. If you are using Visual Basic .NET, you can simply use the Handles keyword after the method name and provide the event that you would like to handle. For example, the following code wires the PutButton_Click event handle with the click event of the button control:

```
Public Sub PutButton_Click(ByVal sender As System.Object, _
            ByVal e As System.EventArgs) Handles PutButton.Click
```

If you are coding in C#, the Handles keyword is not available. You can accomplish the same purpose by writing the following line of code in the InitializeComponent method of the code-behind class:

```
this.AddToCacheButton.Click += new
System.EventHandler(this.AddToCacheButton_Click);
```

Alternatively, you can wire the event handler by using the ASP.NET server control tags. These tags are specified in the .aspx file to represent server controls. Each tag provides a series of attributes that you can use to wire the event handler with events exposed by the server control. Here is an example:

```
<asp:Button id=PutButton OnClick="PutButton_Click" runat="server"
    Text="Put in session" Width="145px"></asp:Button>
```

 CAUTION *C# programmers must be very careful not to double-wire the event handler. You can double-wire an event handler simply by using the ASP.NET server control tag in the .aspx file, as well as by writing appropriate code in the code-behind file. Amazingly enough, Visual Basic .NET is smart enough not to double-wire the event handler even if you do it either by mistake or on purpose. C#, on the other hand, is not that smart.*

Try it out for yourself. Create a C# Web project in Visual Studio .NET and add a button control. Double-click the button control to wire the event handler. Double-clicking a control in Visual Studio .NET causes it to write the appropriate syntax in the code-behind file to wire a handler with the control's click event. Now, switch to the HTML view and add the OnClick attribute to the server control's tag.

You can test your code by setting a break point in the event handler for the click event and watching it get called twice. Now remove either one of the two event handlers, and watch it get called just once.

It took us more than three days to discover why some of the buttons were getting pushed twice every time we clicked them. We hope, by writing down such experiences here, that you won't have to go through such agonizing pains.

Staying Away from the InitializeComponent Method

The InitializeComponent method of the code-behind class is reserved for Visual Studio .NET use only. It's highly recommended that programmers stay away from this method. Visual Studio .NET has a tendency to remove all your custom code from this method, which you won't realize until it's too late.

Try for yourself. Create a Web project by using any programming language. Switch to the code-behind window and write a line of code in the InitializeComponent method. Switch to the design view and either add or remove a server control on the page. Now, switch back to the code-behind view and poof! Your code disappears from the InitializeComponent method. A real-life Lance Burton, Visual Studio .NET is!

Where did our HTML go? If you program with Visual Studio .NET 1.0 long enough, you will find yourself asking this question. This problem occurs when you create ASP.NET Web forms and switch between HTML and design views or when saving the file. Visual Studio .NET can sometimes be too smart for its own good. Its default behavior is to rearrange the HTML that you formatted so precisely. Most programmers desire to write clear code with proper indentation to make it easier to maintain their code later. Few feelings are worse than realizing that all your hard work is thrown out the window because your development tool decided to rearrange your code to its own liking.

You can turn off auto-formatting by choosing Options from the Tools menu. On the Options dialog box, select the Text Editor folder and then select the HTML/XML subfolder. Click Format and clear both the Apply Automatic Formatting checkboxes.

Summary

Web programming has already come a long way since its inception during the mid-1990s. The advent of ASP.NET has made it possible for us to apply traditional and time-tested programming techniques, such as object orientation, event-driven programming, and multitier models, easily and effectively to Web programming.

CHAPTER 2

Cache, Session, and View State

THIS CHAPTER EXPLAINS the intricacies of the three features available in ASP.NET for maintaining state. Each of these features provides a unique solution that comes with its own sets of benefits and problems. Cache, for example, is a very useful mechanism for storing commonly used information in memory. However, cache is not built to support server farms and therefore is best used for nonsession-related information.

Session and view state, on the other hand, are built for session management and can be used across server farms. This chapter focuses on explaining the details of each feature and showing its behavior in a variety of scenarios. You need to understand the capabilities and limitations of each of these features and devise your own magical potion that contains their best combination.

Be Mindful of the Cache!

Caching is a mechanism for keeping content in memory for later use. It helps Web applications operate with higher performance by reducing the amount of work needed to obtain information from its data source, such as a database, Web service, mathematical computation, and many others. ASP.NET provides us with a variety of ways for caching information.

The output cache mechanism keeps rendered pages in memory and serves future requests with the in-memory image of the page. You can customize it and use it to cache different versions of the same page based on the query string values, browser cookies, or form variables.

The data cache mechanism provides us with the ability to store any object in memory and retrieve it at a later time. By using this mechanism, we can access the data source once and keep the result in the memory to serve future requests for the same information.

Cache Pros and Cons

Before you go too wild and start putting everything including the kitchen sink in cache, you need to consider the following benefits and risks.

The benefits include

- A reduced number of round trips to the data source, such as the database server, keeping the server resources more available for other operations.

- An increase in the number of users supported, due to a faster response time to each user's request.

The risks include

- Easily filling a computer's memory, which is relatively small, if you put a large amount of data in cache. As the memory gets full, the performance starts to decline, eventually leading to an unacceptable response time from the server.

- Problems in a server farm environment, when we cache information in the server's memory, where various Web pages for the same user session may be served by different Web servers.

- No guarantee of faster performance. It all depends on how effectively you manage objects in memory. We'll go into more detail on this topic later in this section.

In general, caching is useful when you have a large amount of relatively static information. A prime candidate for caching is product catalog information. There is little value in using SQL to search the database to retrieve the same list of products for each user who visits your Web site. It is a waste of database and network resources (assuming that the database is installed on a separate server than the Web site). You can easily store information like this in data cache. However, before you go wild and put your entire product catalog in one large XML DOM object (or DataSet object), consider this fact: Even though it is easier to get access to an object stored in memory, it is not necessarily faster to search that object.

A prime example of this fact is the DataSet object. The ADO.NET enthusiasts love to glorify this object by focusing on its ability to provide in-memory cache of the database. They often neglect to tell their innocent listeners about the slow performance of its search mechanism. We were surprised when we performance-tested the DataSet search capability and found it to be a much slower alternative to searching a SQL Server 2000 database by using embedded SQL. Let's put the in-memory data caching mechanism to the test. The examples in the following sections demonstrate various strengths and weaknesses related to this mechanism. The purpose of these exercises is merely to show you the realities of technologies involved, not to suggest any one method over another.

NOTE *As suggested at the beginning of this chapter, you should use your best judgment when selecting a data-caching mechanism for your next ASP.NET-based project.*

Performance Testing with Data Caching

Let's have some fun with caching a DataSet object. In this section, we will create a simple ASP.NET application that searches a data store that contains file and directory names. We will call it CacheBuster. This application will be capable of keeping the in-memory copy of the database and using it to search for required information. For comparison's sake, we will also create a mechanism for searching a SQL Server 2000 database by using embedded SQL to retrieve the same information.

The schema of the table contained in the SQL Server 2000 database is shown in Table 2-1. It contains roughly 50,000 records. It may seem like a lot of data, but it is not uncommon for a Web application to process this amount of information. A successful eCommerce site can easily have more than 50,000 customer records, order records, SKU records, etc.

Table 2-1. CacheBuster Database Table Schema

TABLE NAME	COLUMN NAME	DATA TYPE
Files	Id	Numeric
Files	FileName	Varchar(255)
Files	DirectoryName	Varchar(255)

The first thing we'll do is store the data in cache.

Storing Data in Cache

Use the Page_Load event to check whether the DataSet object is available in cache or not. If it is not, use embedded SQL and the ADO.NET framework to create a new DataSet object and store it in cache. Listing 2-1 shows C# code for storing data in cache.

Listing 2-1. C# Code for Storing Data in Cache

```csharp
private void Page_Load(object sender, System.EventArgs e)
{
    // If the DataSet object is not in cache, get it
    // from the database.
    if (Cache["Result"] == null)
    {
        SqlCommand MyCommand = new SqlCommand();
        MyCommand.Connection =  new SqlConnection("your connection string");
        MyCommand.CommandText = " select * from files ";

        SqlDataAdapter MyAdapter = new SqlDataAdapter();
        MyAdapter.SelectCommand = MyCommand;

        DataSet MyDataSet = new DataSet();

        // Retreiving result set from the database and populating
        // DataSet with it.
        MyCommand.Connection.Open();
        MyAdapter.Fill(MyDataSet);
        MyConnection.Close();

        MyAdapter.SelectCommand.Dispose();
        MyAdapter.Dispose();

        // Placing the DataSet object in cache.
        Cache["Result"] = MyDataSet;
    }
}
```

Let's look at the user interface for the CacheBuster application, shown in Figure 2-1. You will see that it contains a text box that receives the name of the directory you want to search. By using this name, it can find all the files in that directory by using the in-memory cached DataSet object. Alternatively, it can also search for all files in the given directory by running a SQL statement on a SQL Server database.

Directory Name :

Figure 2-1. *User interface for the CacheBuster application*

Searching DataSet

Let's look at the code that uses the DataSet's built-in search mechanism. In Listing 2-2, we use the DataView object to filter rows contained in a DataTable object. The RowFilter property of the DataView object receives an expression similar to the WHERE clause of a SQL statement. By using this filter, the DataView object uses the Select method of the DataTable object to perform the search.

BEST PRACTICE *Why not use the Select method of the DataTable object directly? The problem with the Select method is that it returns an array of DataRow objects. It is not easy to bind this array to a server control because the System.Array class doesn't implement the IListSource and IList interfaces. It is better to use the DataView object to bind a set of DataRow objects to a server control.*

On the other hand, if you need to filter a data table for reasons other than binding to a control, you are better off using DataTable's Select method directly. This way, you don't incur the overhead associated with the DataView object. Listing 2-2 shows how to search a cached DataSet object.

Listing 2-2. *Searching a Cached DataSet Object*

```
private void DirectoryFromCacheButton_Click(object sender, System.EventArgs e)
{
    if (Cache["Result"] == null)
        return;
```

```
DateTime StartTime, EndTime;
TimeSpan Duration;

// Retrieving DataSet object from cache.
DataSet MyDataSet = Cache["Result"] as DataSet;

// Starting to measure time.
StartTime = DateTime.Now;

// Creating DataView object, which will be filtered and bound
// to the data grid control.
DataView MyDataView = new DataView(MyDataSet.Tables[0]);
MyDataView.RowFilter = " DirectoryName = '" + DirectoryTextBox.Text + "' ";

ResultGrid.DataSource = MyDataView;
ResultGrid.DataBind();

// Stopping time measurement.
EndTime = DateTime.Now;

Duration = EndTime - StartTime;

CacheLabel.Text = "Searched cached DataSet object";

// Displaying elapsed time on the screen.
DurationLabel.Text = Duration.Milliseconds.ToString() + " milliseconds ";
}
```

When we ran CacheBuster and measured the time it took for the DataSet to filter the desired rows, we got the result shown in Figure 2-2. The test was conducted on an 850 MHz PC with 256 MB of RAM.

Directory Name :

| Directory from Cache |
| Directory from Database |

debug

Searched cached DataSet object

380 milliseconds

Id	FileName	DirectoryName
2139	WindowsApplication1.exe	Debug
2140	WindowsApplication1.pdb	Debug
2141	WindowsApplication1.exe	Debug
2142	WindowsApplication1.exe.incr	Debug
2143	WindowsApplication1.Form1.resources	Debug
2144	WindowsApplication1.pdb	Debug

Figure 2-2. The execution time for filtering the DataSet for the desired rows

Searching by Using a SQL Server Database

Now that we know that it takes 380 milliseconds to filter a data table of 50,000 records, let's perform the same operation by using a SQL Server 2000 database. Listing 2-1 showed how we used the ADO.NET framework to perform a Select query on a SQL Server database; Listing 2-3 shows the code to extract data from the database and to bind it to the data grid control.

Listing 2-3. C# Code for Searching the SQL Server Database

```csharp
private void DirectoryFromDBButton_Click(object sender, System.EventArgs e)
{
    DateTime StartTime, EndTime;
    TimeSpan Duration;

    DataSet MyDataSet = new DataSet();
    SqlDataAdapter MyAdapter = new SqlDataAdapter();
    SqlCommand MyCommand = new SqlCommand();
    MyCommand.Connection = new SqlConnection("your connection string");

    // Specifying SQL SELECT statement using WHERE clause to
    // filter the result by matching directory name.
    MyCommand.CommandText = " select * from files where DirectoryName = '" +
                    DirectoryTextBox.Text + "' ";
```

```
// Starting to measure time.
StartTime = DateTime.Now;

MyAdapter.SelectCommand = MyCommand;
MyCommand.Connection.Open();

// Filling data set with results return from SQL query.
MyAdapter.Fill(MyDataSet);

ResultGrid.DataSource = MyDataSet.Tables[0].DefaultView;
ResultGrid.DataBind();

// Ending time measurement.
EndTime = DateTime.Now;

MyCommand.Connection.Close();
MyCommand.Dispose();

Duration = EndTime - StartTime;

CacheLabel.Text = "Searched SQL Server 2000 Database";

// Displaying elapsed time on the screen.
DurationLabel.Text = Duration.Milliseconds.ToString() + " milliseconds ";
}
```

Let's run CacheBuster again and see the performance measurement. Figure 2-3 shows the execution time that results from performing the SQL Select query against a SQL Server 2000 database.

You can clearly see that searching the database only took 90 milliseconds, which is roughly four times faster than using a cached DataSet object. One would wonder why to bother with memory cache when it doesn't provide the performance increase for which one hoped. Before you throw away your data caching code and revert to writing SQL for all your data needs, let us explain why caching can still be a better option. We will also show you how to optimize memory cache for better performance.

Directory Name :

| debug |

Directory from Cache

Directory from Database

Searched SQL Server 2000 Database

90 milliseconds

Id	FileName	DirectoryName
2139	WindowsApplication1.exe	Debug
2140	WindowsApplication1.pdb	Debug
2141	WindowsApplication1.exe	Debug
2142	WindowsApplication1.exe.incr	Debug
2143	WindowsApplication1.Form1.resources	Debug
2144	WindowsApplication1.pdb	Debug

Figure 2-3. The execution time for performing SQL Select statement

When Good Cache Goes Bad

The performance problems we just saw didn't occur because we chose to put a relatively large amount of data in memory. The problems also didn't occur because the server ran out of available memory and had to resort to using virtual memory. This performance problem arises because the DataView object doesn't seem to be optimized for performance. This problem becomes evident when you use this object on a data table that contains more than 20,000 records. Depending on the speed of your hardware, you might even see this problem with data table that contains fewer records.

Still, you can use a few tricks to get better performance while searching cached data. One such trick is to restructure the data to make it more fragmented.

Restructuring the Data Set

In our next example, we will modify the data set to include another data table with the name "Directories." This data table will contain only directory names. We will also create a relationship between two tables to link matching directory names. Figure 2-4 shows the data model that shows both the Directories and the Files tables.

Figure 2-4. Modified data set structure

Including the Directories data table allows for a quick search for the directory name. Because this data table contains only unique directory names, it has much fewer records than the Files table. When a matching directory is found, we can use the relationship to retrieve all files contained in the directory from the Files data table.

Listing 2-4. Making the Code Modifications to Show an Increase in Performance

```
private void Page_Load(object sender, System.EventArgs e)
{
    if (Cache["Result"] == null)
    {
        SqlCommand MyCommand = new SqlCommand();
        MyCommand.Connection =  new SqlConnection("your connection string");
        MyCommand.CommandText = " select * from files ";

        SqlDataAdapter MyAdapter = new SqlDataAdapter();
        MyAdapter.SelectCommand = MyCommand;

        DataSet MyFastDataSet = new DataSet();

        MyCommand.Connection.Open();

        // Adding Files table to the data set.
        MyAdapter.Fill(MyFastDataSet, "Files");

        // Selecting unique directory name from the database.
        MyCommand.CommandText = " select Distinct DirectoryName from Files ";

        // Adding Directories table to the data set.
        MyAdapter.Fill(MyFastDataSet, "Directories");

        DataColumn ParentColumn =
        MyFastDataSet.Tables["Directories"].Columns["DirectoryName"];
        DataColumn ChildColumn =
        MyFastDataSet.Tables["Files"].Columns["DirectoryName"];
```

```
        // Creating a relationship between Directories and Files
        // data tables.
        MyFastDataSet.Relations.Add("Directory_File_Relation",
                            ParentColumn, ChildColumn);

        MyConnection.Close();
        MyAdapter.SelectCommand.Dispose();
        MyAdapter.Dispose();

        // Adding data set to cache
        Cache["FastResult"] = MyFastDataSet;
    }
}


// This method runs when user clicks Directory from Cache button.
private void DirectoryFromCacheButton_Click(object sender, System.EventArgs e)
{
    if (Cache["FastResult"] == null)
        return;

    DateTime StartTime, EndTime;
    TimeSpan Duration;

    DataSet MyFastDataSet = Cache["FastResult"] as DataSet;

    string DirectoryFilter = " DirectoryName = '" + DirectoryTextBox.Text + "' ";

    // Starting measuring time.
    StartTime = DateTime.Now;

    DataView DirectoryView =  new
DataView(MyFastDataSet.Tables["Directories"]);

    // Filtering Directories table for the raw matching input
    // directory name.
    DirectoryView.RowFilter = DirectoryFilter;

    if (DirectoryView.Count == 0)
        return;

    // Using the relationship to find all files matching
    // directory name.
    DataView FilesView =
        DirectoryView[0].CreateChildView("Directory_File_Relation");
```

```
ResultGrid.DataSource = FilesView;
ResultGrid.DataBind();

// Stopping time measurement.
EndTime = DateTime.Now;

Duration = EndTime - StartTime;

CacheLabel.Text = "Searched cached Fast DataSet object";
DurationLabel.Text = Duration.Milliseconds.ToString() +  " milliseconds ";
}
```

Just by creating the Directories data table, we are able to reduce the time it took to search for files by roughly 30 percent, as shown by the snapshot view in Figure 2-5.

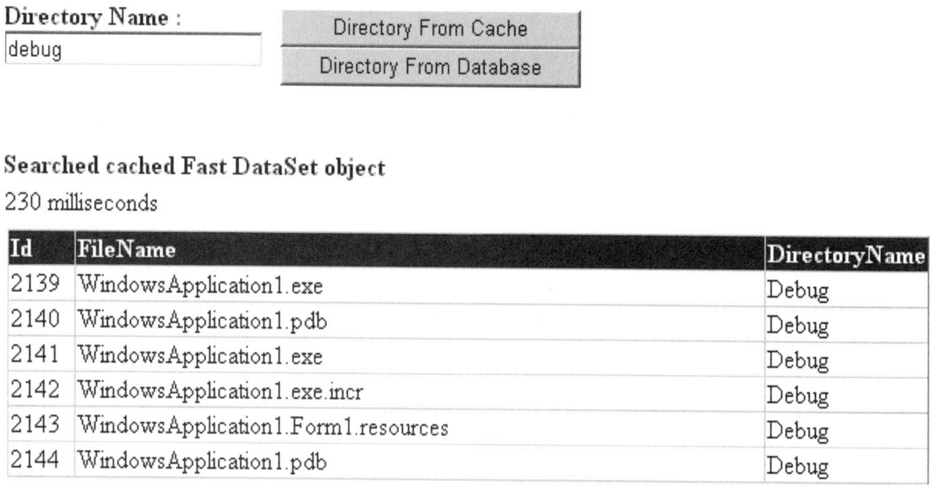

Directory Name :

| debug |

| Directory From Cache |
| Directory From Database |

Searched cached Fast DataSet object

230 milliseconds

Id	FileName	DirectoryName
2139	WindowsApplication1.exe	Debug
2140	WindowsApplication1.pdb	Debug
2141	WindowsApplication1.exe	Debug
2142	WindowsApplication1.exe.incr	Debug
2143	WindowsApplication1.Form1.resources	Debug
2144	WindowsApplication1.pdb	Debug

Figure 2-5. The execution time for searching the data set by using the restructured data set

It's Still Too Slow!

You might not be a happy camper because all our work didn't provide a dramatic increase in performance. You might be curious why you should bother caching your data when you can retrieve it from the SQL Server within 90 milliseconds, as compared with 380 milliseconds from a regular data set cache or 230 milliseconds from the so-called fast data set cache.

There are, however, the following advantages of using the in-memory data cache:

- Keeping data in memory keeps your database available for more business-critical transactions. For example, an eCommerce site processes large amounts of data to display information to the users. Information such as product catalog, pricing, promotion, etc. doesn't change very often. Keeping the database available for critical business transactions, such as order processing, order fulfillment, and merchandising, contributes significantly to running business processes smoothly.

- Keeping data in memory also reduces network traffic on your network. Most Web sites use a separate server for keeping their database. If you make a trip to the database for all your data needs, you will generate a large amount of network traffic.

 BEST PRACTICE *Keeping less-dynamic and often-used data in cache keeps the database and network available for other important processes. Architecturally, you will have to accept a slight degradation in performance for higher availability of these critical components.*

Refreshing Cached Data

The ASP.NET framework doesn't provide an elaborate mechanism for refreshing cached data if it is changed in the database. You can probably rig something to make it work. You can perhaps create an assembly and register it as a COM component by using the Regasm.exe tool. Once the assembly is registered as a COM component, you can fire a trigger on the database update to call a stored procedure that can invoke your assembly as a COM object. In your assembly, you can clear out the cache. The ASP.NET framework, however, does provide an elegant mechanism for receiving notification if the data is stored in a file instead of in the database. We would recommend that you consider keeping your cache candidate data in an XML file. While you develop designs for your system, you should determine which kinds of information make good candidates for caching. There are no hard and fast rules on finding such information. Each application is unique with its own set of data requirements. The general rule of thumb is to recognize the information that changes less frequently and needs to be presented consistently for every user.

You can export data from the database into an XML file fairly easily. All you have to do is to create a DataSet object by running one or many SQL statements. The data adapter object provides the flexibility of executing multiple SELECT commands and populating more than one data table from their result sets. Once you have filled all needed data tables, make sure to create appropriate relationships. These relationships will help you greatly when you attempt to filter the information contained in the data set. After creating the DataSet object, you can simply call its WriteXML method to save its content to an XML file.

Extracting Data from a Database and Saving It into an XML File

Listing 2-5 shows how to extract data from a database and save it to an XML file. It starts by creating a DataSet object by using multiple SQL statements and persistence of its content in an XML file.

Listing 2-5. Data Persistence in an XML File

```
string XmlFileName;
SqlCommand MyCommand = new SqlCommand();

MyCommand.Connection = new SqlConnection("your connection string");
MyCommand.CommandText = " select * from files ";

SqlDataAdapter MyAdapter = new SqlDataAdapter();
MyAdapter.SelectCommand = MyCommand;

DataSet MyFastDataSet = new DataSet();

MyCommand.Connection.Open();

// Filling one table in the data set.
MyAdapter.Fill(MyFastDataSet, "Files");

MyCommand.CommandText = " select Distinct DirectoryName from Files ";

// Filling another table in the data set.
MyAdapter.Fill(MyFastDataSet, "Directories");

DataColumn ParentColumn =
  MyFastDataSet.Tables["Directories"].Columns["DirectoryName"];
DataColumn ChildColumn = MyFastDataSet.Tables["Files"].Columns["DirectoryName"];

// Creating relationship between both tables.
MyFastDataSet.Relations.Add("Directory_File_Relation", ParentColumn,
ChildColumn);
```

```
MyConnection.Close();
MyAdapter.SelectCommand.Dispose();
MyAdapter.Dispose();


// Using MapPath method to get physical file path for virtual
// file location.
XmlFileName = Request.MapPath("CacheFile/MyFastDataSet.xml");


// Saving data set content to an XML file. The WriteSchema
// enumeration is used to cause the data set to write schema,
// as well as, content.
MyFastDataSet.WriteXml(XmlFileName, XmlWriteMode.WriteSchema);


// Disposing DataSet because we don't need it anymore.
MyFastDataSet.Dispose();
```

BEST PRACTICE *We recommend using the DataSet object to create the XML file if you are planning to use the data set to cache information.*

Yes, you can create the XML file by using a variety of mechanisms, including the SQL Server 2000 built-in XML generation features. However, in our experience, we have found it easier to convert an XML file to a data set if the file was originated from a DataSet object.

Also, make sure to write the schema to the file as well. Without writing the schema, you will lose important column-level information, such as data type. Without saving the schema, you will also lose relationships between tables, which is sure to cost you several hours of debugging to discover the real cause of the problem.

Losing a column's data type isn't much fun either. It will start to affect you when you try to sort the column by using the DataView object. Because the column won't know its data type, it will default to string, resulting in alphanumeric sorting for numeric information. Believe us, no customer likes to see alphanumeric sorting for phone numbers or dates. We have been burned on this one. Once you have saved data in an XML file by using the DataSet object, it is very easy to convert it back into a data set. In fact, it is as simple as calling the ReadXML method on the DataSet object and providing it with the name and the location of the XML file. The trick, however, is to update the cache correctly. Some of you may be thinking, what's so hard about updating cache? You simply get the data set from cache and call its ReadXML method.

CAUTION *Never ever, we repeat, never ever directly update the cached DataSet object from the XML file.*

When you are ready to refresh cache, make sure to create a new DataSet object and populate it by calling its ReadXML method. Once the new DataSet object is populated, throw away the current DataSet object that is residing in cache and insert the newly created DataSet object in its place.

The reason you shouldn't use the currently cached DataSet object to refresh data is that the ReadXML method can take up to several minutes if the XML file is large. Of course, you don't want to affect users who are innocently surfing your Web site by silently pulling the rug from under their feet (or updating their data as they are using it).

Populating a new DataSet object from an XML file doesn't affect Web site users. You should still be careful while overwriting cache with the new object. Even though it only takes a fraction of a second to place a new DataSet object in cache, it is best to synchronize access to the Cache object while performing this operation.

Refreshing a Cached DataSet Object

Make sure to read the code in Listing 2-6 to see an example of how to refresh cache appropriately. It uses the lock keyword to synchronize all threads that are trying to access the cache to make sure that only one thread gets to update it at a time. Because the ASP.NET runtime engine processes each Web request as a separate thread, this logic causes all Web requests that are trying to access cache to synchronize while it is being updated.

Listing 2-6. An Example of Refreshing Cache Appropriately

```
// Using MapPath method to convert virtual file path to physical path.
string XmlFileName = Request.MapPath("CacheFile/MyFastDataSet.xml");

// Creating new DataSet object.
DataSet MyFastDataSet = new DataSet();

// Populating newly created DataSet object from XML file.
// Make sure to use ReadSchema enumeration; otherwise,
// the DataSet object will not have data types and relations.
MyFastDataSet.ReadXml(XmlFileName, XmlReadMode.ReadSchema);
```

```
// Synchronize access to the Cache object by using the lock keyword.
// The lock keyword makes sure that no other thread can access the
// Cache object while it's being updated with new DataSet object.
lock(Cache)
{
Cache["Result"] = MyFastDataSet;
}
```

Expiring Cache

The caching mechanism provides us with the flexibility of expiring cached data by using a variety of methods. You can make a cached object dependent on a specific file. If the file changes, the caching mechanism will be notified and will expunge the cached object from the memory. Similarly, you can make a cached object dependent on a directory. If any change is made to that directory or any of its subdirectories, the object will be expunged from cache. You can make various cached objects dependent on each other, in which case, when a cached object is expired, all its dependent cached objects expire as well. The caching mechanism also provides us with the ability to make cached objects expire after a certain time interval. We are free to specify either a fixed time or a sliding duration.

The CacheItemRemovedCallback Delegate

Another nice feature provided by the caching mechanism is its ability to notify us when our objects are removed from cache. This notification is done by using the CacheItemRemovedCallback delegate, which is defined in the System.Web.Caching namespace. By using this delegate, we can receive the expired cached object, its key name, and a reason for the expiration.

 BEST PRACTICE *If you use an XML file to load a data set in memory and keep it cached, we recommend that you set the dependency of your cached data set with that file.*

By using this mechanism, your code can receive notification when the file is changed. Once you receive such notification, you can read this recently updated file, create a new DataSet object, and replace the cached object with it.

This approach allows you to refresh the data simply by updating the underlying XML file and to let the ASP.NET runtime and its caching mechanism do the rest.

Listing 2-7 shows how you can set up dependency with a file, receive expiration notification, and set various expiration options.

Listing 2-7. Setting Up Dependency with a File

```
// Make sure to include System.Web.Caching namespace.
private void AddToCache()
{
    // Using MapPath method to convert virtual file path to physical path.
    string XmlFileName = Request.MapPath("CacheFile/MyFastDataSet.xml");

    // Creating new DataSet object.
    DataSet MyFastDataSet = new DataSet();

    // Populating newly created DataSet object
    // from XML file. Make sure to use ReadSchema
    // enumeration; otherwise, the DataSet object will not
    // have data types and relations.
    MyFastDataSet.ReadXml(XmlFileName, XmlReadMode.ReadSchema);

    CacheDependency MyDependency;
    CacheItemRemovedCallback onRemove;

    // Setting the dependency object to the XML file.
    MyDependency = new CacheDependency(XmlFileName);

    // Creating the delegate object and assigning it the
    // name of the method that should be called when cached
    // data set is expired.
    onRemove = new CacheItemRemovedCallback(RemoveResultCallback);

    // Inserting the newly created DataSet object in cache
    // and assigning it the dependency, the delegate, and expiration
    // values. In this example, the cached data set will expire
    // 24 hours after it is placed in cache.
    Cache.Insert("Result", MyFastDataSet, MyDependency,
        DateTime.Now.AddHours(24),
        TimeSpan.Zero, CacheItemPriority.Normal, onRemove);
}


// This method will be called when the cached data set is expunged.
// It receives the expired object, its key, and the reason for
// expiration as specified in CacheItemRemovedCallback delegate.
private void RemoveResultCallback(string key, object removedObject,
        CacheItemRemovedReason removeReason)
```

```
{
    // We simply call the AddToCache() method to reread the
    // XML file and refresh cached data set.
    AddToCache();
}
```

The Cache object provides a method called Add. We tend to stay away from using this method. We have yet to understand the reason for this method. Its existence seems redundant and, quite frankly, annoying. The Add method works in the same manner as the Insert method, but it returns the object you just inserted in cache, which is the part that we have yet to comprehend. Why would you want to receive the object you just provided to this method as a parameter? You already have it, don't you? Even if you receive the returned object, you lose all your type information because the returned object is of the generic type "object." The Add method also throws exceptions if you try to add an item with the key name that already exists. As a best practice, we recommend that you always check to see if another object uses the same key name before you use that key for your object. We recommend that you perform your own checks prior to using the Insert method instead of using the Add method, and handle exceptions as they happen.

Understanding the CacheDependency Class

The CacheDependency class is very versatile. With this class, you can set the expiration of your cached object by using a variety of mechanisms, from sensing file changes to the expiration of another cached object. This class doesn't expose many properties; rather, it relies on you to provide appropriate information in its constructor. By using one of its eight overloaded constructors, you can configure this object to create a dependency between your cached object and any number of files, directories, and other cached objects. You can even specify the date and time when you would like the dependency to take effect.

NOTE   *When you use the delegate to receive cache expiration notification, the object representing the page stays in memory until the cache is purged. Normally, the ASP.NET Page objects are created for each request and destroyed after the request is processed. However, when the Cache object holds a reference to a method on the Page object, the Page object needs to stay instantiated. Otherwise, the Cache object may end up with a null reference in its delegate. The Page object, however, is not reused to process any more Web requests; it stays in memory, waiting to receive the callback from the Cache object.*

Losing Cached Information When Restarting the Application

It is important for you to know that the Cache object keeps its content in the memory of the Web application. If the Web application restarts for any reason, it loses its cached objects. A Web application can restart in many ways, some that you might already know and some that may surprise you. One way a Web application restarts is when the Web server is restarted, which can happen either accidentally or deliberately. However, the Web application also restarts if any change is made in either the Web.config or the Machine.config file. The ASP.NET runtime senses changes to its configuration files and starts a new application domain that loads the changed configuration file in memory. The new application domain creates its own Cache object, causing us to lose objects stored in the previous application domain's cache.

This behavior is the classic example of the compromises that are made in the ASP.NET framework for providing other, more needed, benefits. The ASP.NET framework designers wanted a mechanism for configuring Web applications that does not depend on Windows registry. The alternative was to use XML-based configuration files. However, reading configuration from file I/O can be fairly intense and may become the performance bottleneck in high-use scenarios. The ASP.NET runtime designers chose to read the configuration files once, when the Web application starts, and keep its information cached in memory. They also used the file dependency feature to sense changes made to the configuration files. Once a file change is detected, the ASP.NET runtime does not update the configuration information cached in the memory and instead creates a new application domain. The benefit of creating a new application domain is that all existing Web requests can continue to use the existing configuration and new Web requests are diverted to the new application domain. The disadvantage of creating a new application domain is that it doesn't bring the cached objects from the previous application domain and results in empty cache.

The Scalability Issue with Cached Objects

As we mentioned earlier, the cached objects are stored in the Web application memory, which can cause problems in the Web farm environment. It is not uncommon for high-traffic Web sites to use multiple Web servers. Often a load balancer is used to divert the incoming Web request to the least busy Web server. Because cached objects are stored in the Web application's memory, they are not accessible from another server in the farm, which results in unpredictable behavior, as there is no good way of knowing which server in the farm will be used to process the request. Usually when someone talks about scalability problems with a given technology, the conversation follows with bad publicity, expert opinions on what should have been, and the tendency of developers to stay away from using the technology. On the contrary, we are here to tell you that the scalability problem with the Cache object is a wonderful thing. But before we tell you why, let us also say that if you are experiencing a scalability problem with the Cache object, you built your application wrong.

BEST PRACTICE   *The Cache object is not meant for keeping user-specific information.*

If you are keeping information pertaining to a specific user in the Cache object, you built your Web application wrong. The purpose of the Cache object is to store information available to all users of your Web application. If you need to keep user-specific information in memory, you should use the Session object instead.

If the information in the Cache object is not usercentric, then you don't have to worry about maintaining any specific user's session across the server farm.

You should always provide a mechanism for retrieving information from the physical store, such as the database, if the cache is found empty. Standardizing on this logic helps you to scale your application in a server farm environment. If a specific server in the farm doesn't have your cached information, your application will retrieve it from the physical store and add it to the cache. Eventually, all servers in the farm will have retrieved the cached information.

Some of you may wonder why the ASP.NET framework doesn't provide the ability to scale the Cache object by using either a state server or relational database, similar to the way the Session object can be scaled. The answer is quite simple: There are significant performance implications in keeping information in a state server or a database session. The performance degradation can be justified in the case of the Session object because of its ability to maintain usercentric information across multiple servers in the farm. On the other hand, the performance penalty can't be justified for information that does not pertain to a specific user of the Web application. If you are skeptical about the performance issues with the state server and database sessions, make sure to read the section "Understanding the Session Object" later in this chapter.

Turbo-Charging with Output Caching

Output caching can boost the performance of your Web application by multiple orders of magnitude. We highly recommend every one of you to pay close attention to the scenarios in which output caching can be a viable option.

The rule of thumb is to select pages that are used very often and don't change much. A really cool feature of the ASP.NET output caching mechanism is its ability to generate different cached versions of the same page based on a variety of input parameters, such as query string values, form post values, etc. This feature provides us with the ability to generate different cached outputs for different users of our site. You can keep the user ID either embedded in the query string or as a hidden field on the page. You can then use the VaryByParam attribute to cache different page outputs for each user. It is as simple as adding the following line of code at the beginning of the .aspx file.

```
<%@ OutputCache Duration="60" VaryByParam="UserId" %>
```

If you are not so inclined to keep the user ID in a query string or a hidden field, you can always keep it in a cookie and use the VaryByCustom attribute to accomplish the same purpose.

```
<%@ OutputCache Duration="60" VaryByCustom="UserId" %>
```

The UserId parameter doesn't exist, but the VaryByCustom attribute allows you create it by writing a few lines of code in the GetVaryByCustomString method in the Global.asax file. In this method, you can write the following line of code to cache different outputs for each user of your site.

```
public override string GetVaryByCustomString(HttpContext Context, string Args)
{
    return "UserId=" + Request.Cookies["UserIdCookie"].Value;
}
```

A good candidate for output caching is the home page of your Web application. In most applications, the home page is the most visited page. If the home page for your application is dynamically generated, we highly recommend that you consider enabling output caching on this page. If your home page doesn't show different content to different users, all you have to do is to write the following line of code at the beginning of the page:

```
<%@ OutputCache Duration="3600" VaryByParam="None" %>
```

The previously mentioned code will cause your home page to be cached for one hour (3,600 seconds). By setting the VaryByParam attribute to None, you can specify that this page should appear the same for all users of your site. If you need to show different versions of the home page to different users, you can use any of the techniques mentioned previously.

Another good candidate for output caching are pages that show product catalogs, search results, navigation links, etc. In fact, with a little creativity, you can even cache pictures and PDF files. Keep reading and you will find out how.

If you don't believe that output caching can turbo-boost your Web application, let me prove it to you with code examples and concrete performance test results. In Listing 2-8, we will create a simple page that retrieves some data from a SQL Server database and shows it on the screen. We will then use Application Center to performance-test this page with and without output caching. All you nonbelievers tag along with us and see for yourselves.

Listing 2-8. Retrieving Some Data from the SQL Server Database

```
private void Page_Load(object sender, System.EventArgs e
{
    SqlCommand MyCommand = new SqlCommand();
    MyCommand.Connection = new SqlConnection("Your Connection String");

    // Selecting 100 records from the database.
    MyCommand.CommandText = " select top 100 * from files ";

    SqlDataAdapter MyAdapter = new SqlDataAdapter();
    MyAdapter.SelectCommand = MyCommand;

    // Filling a data set with result from SQL query.
    DataSet MyDataSet = new DataSet();

    MyCommand.Connection.Open();
    MyAdapter.Fill(MyDataSet, "Files");
    MyCommand.Connection.Close();

    MyAdapter.SelectCommand.Dispose();
    MyAdapter.Dispose();

    // Showing the content from data set in the data grid control.
    ResultGrid.DataSource = MyDataSet.Tables[0].DefaultView;
    ResultGrid.DataBind();
}
```

When you compile and run this code, you will see the page shown in Figure 2-6.

Id	FileName	DirectoryName
257	AUTOEXEC.BAT	c:\
258	boot.ini	c:\
259	BOOTLOG.TXT	c:\
260	CONFIG.SYS	c:\
261	hiberfil.sys	c:\
262	HPSUPPT.TXT	c:\
263	IO.SYS	c:\
264	MSDOS.SYS	c:\
265	NTDETECT.COM	c:\

Figure 2-6. The page that demonstrates output caching

Let's create three versions of this page. The first version will not use any output caching, the second version will use client output caching, and the third version will use the server output caching.

The client output caching option caches the page at the browser, whereas the server output caching option caches it at the Web server. You will find the performance difference between these two options in Listing 2-9 and Figure 2-7.

Listing 2-9. The HTML Contained in the .aspx File for All Three Output Caching Options

```
<!-- HTML for no output caching -->
<%@ Page language="c#" Codebehind="OutputCaching-None.aspx.cs"
AutoEventWireup="false" Inherits="ASPNET.OutputCaching___None" %>
<HTML>
  <HEAD><title>OutputCaching - None</title></HEAD>
  <body MS_POSITIONING="GridLayout">
    <form id="OutputCaching_None" method="post" runat="server">
<asp:datagrid id=ResultGrid style="Z-INDEX: 103; LEFT: 8px;
POSITION: absolute; TOP: 8px" runat="server">
<HeaderStyle Font-Bold="True" ForeColor="White" BackColor="Blue">
</HeaderStyle></asp:datagrid>
      </form></body>
</HTML>


<!-- HTML for client output caching -->
<%@ OutputCache Duration="10" VaryByParam="None" Location="Client" %>
<%@ Page language="c#" Codebehind="OutputCaching-Client.aspx.cs"
AutoEventWireup="false" Inherits="ASPNET.OutputCaching" %>
```

```
<HTML>
  <HEAD><title>OutputCaching</title></HEAD>
  <body MS_POSITIONING="GridLayout">
    <form id="OutputCaching" method="post" runat="server">
<asp:datagrid id=ResultGrid style="Z-INDEX: 103; LEFT: 16px;
POSITION: absolute; TOP: 30px" runat="server">
<HeaderStyle Font-Bold="True" ForeColor="White" BackColor="Blue">
</HeaderStyle></asp:datagrid></form></body>
</HTML>


<!-- HTML for server output caching -->
<%@ OutputCache Duration="10" VaryByParam="None" Location="Server" %>
<%@ Page language="c#" Codebehind="OutputCaching-Server.aspx.cs"
AutoEventWireup="false" Inherits="ASPNET.OutputCaching__Server" %>
<HTML>
  <HEAD>
    <title>OutputCaching - Server</title>
  </HEAD>
  <body MS_POSITIONING="GridLayout">
    <form id="OutputCaching_Server" method="post" runat="server">
<asp:datagrid id=ResultGrid style="Z-INDEX: 103; LEFT: 8px;
POSITION: absolute; TOP: 8px" runat="server">
<HeaderStyle Font-Bold="True" ForeColor="White" BackColor="Blue">
</HeaderStyle></asp:datagrid></form></body>
</HTML>
```

We created Application Center test scripts that run each of these pages for 10 seconds simulating 10 simultaneous users. Application Center is a performance testing tool that ships with the enterprise architect version of Visual Studio .NET. It helps us to create test scripts to test Web sites for performance. The graph in Figure 2-7 shows the result.

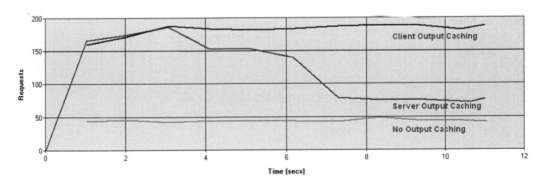

Figure 2-7. Performance test result from Application Center test scripts

Figure 2-7 clearly shows that the page that used output caching ran signifi-cantly faster than the page that didn't use it. Wondering why the page with the Server Output Caching option gradually slowed down as time went by? The slow-down happened because the Web server wasn't able to handle this many simultaneous users. This decline in performance is related to the capability of the hardware.

This is precisely the reason why the page with the Client Output Caching option demonstrated such good performance. It didn't need to make a trip back to the server. Instead, it used its local cached output.

BEST PRACTICE *Output caching is the turbo-charger for your Web application. Use it anywhere you possibly can.*

Deciding Whether to Maintain View State

In the good old days of ASP programming, most of us occasionally created a hid-den field on the Web page for the sole purpose of retaining information during roundtrips to the server. The ASP.NET design team at Microsoft realized the importance of this mechanism and provided us with an easy to use and safe mechanism to accomplish the same purpose.

View state is simply an encoded piece of information that is written in a hid-den field in the Web page. You can add any information you want to the view state by using the following syntax:

```
ViewState["MyName"] = "Farhan Muhammad";
```

Just like Cache and Session, ViewState is also a name/value collection. You can put any information in it and associate it with a key name. When the page is rendered, the information contained in the ViewState name/value collection is written in a hidden field named __VIEWSTATE. The structure and the content of this field are shown in the following code. Notice that the content of this field is encoded and therefore relatively safe from prying eyes.

```
<input type="hidden" name="__VIEWSTATE"
value="dDwtMTI3OTMzNDM4NDtOPHA8bDxNeU5hbWU7PjtsPEZhcmhhbiBNdWhhbW1hZ
Ds+Pjs7Pjs+hVkdc10kDgvCSLOkCPMvlbKn5Yk=" />
```

The server controls also use view state to maintain their state. As you know, a key benefit of using ASP.NET server controls is their ability to retain their con-tent during post-back events. This ability enables the programmers to focus their time and energy on providing business values and not in writing plumbing code.

As simple as it seems, the view state can quickly become evil and can tax your network to its limits.

The data bound server controls, such as drop-down lists, check box lists, data grid, repeater, etc., by default will persist their data to the view state hidden field. All that information ends up traveling from the browser to the server during each post-back event.

We would recommend using either Session or Cache object to store database-generated information and rebinding your controls on each post-back. The performance difference between maintaining view state and rebinding controls from cache is negligible. However, reduced view state size results in a lower amount of information travel from browser to the server, resulting in better throughput.

On the other hand, storing information in cache taxes memory use. However, we would prefer to be taxed on memory rather than network resources. Internet-enabled applications rely on third-party networks to facilitate communication between the browser PC and the server PC. The geographic distance between these computers could be significant, resulting in many hops before the information gets to its destination.

 BEST PRACTICE *As a rule of thumb, we would recommend reducing view state size by setting the EnableViewState property of the server controls to false. You can store the information in either session or cache and rebind your server controls on each post-back.*

This approach results in higher memory use on the server but reduces the amount of information that travels across the Internet to reach its destination. In a high-traffic environment, you are sure to get better throughput by using this approach.

There is one caveat, though. If you choose to disable view state and use the server's memory to remember the information, then you won't be able to discover whether the user changed the information before the post-back event occurred. The ASP.NET runtime uses view state to discover if the user changed the value of the control and fired the OnChange event if necessary. In the absence of view state, ASP.NET runtime tries to compare the value of a control received during post-back with the value of the control declaratively assigned in the HTML, which could cause the OnChange event always to fire if the control's value is different than its default value. This method is more applicable to input type controls, such as text box. Needless to say, such behaviors can be very difficult to discover and debug. In light of such issues, we recommend the following caution associated with disabling view state.

CAUTION *If you need to capture a server-side OnChange event from a particular control, make sure to leave view state enabled. Otherwise, you may consider disabling it to reduce the page size.*

View State: Behind the Scenes

It is important for you to understand the mechanism that makes view state possible. Every time a page is requested from the Web server, the ASP.NET runtime creates a new object of the Page class. This object receives all input values from the request, reads the hidden __VIEWSTATE field, decrypts its content, and uses it to populate the values of appropriate server controls. This process is called server controls rehydration.

After the request is finished processing on the server, the Page object is destroyed. Before the Page object is destroyed, however, the server controls are given an opportunity to store their information in the hidden __VIEWSTATE field. This process is called server controls dehydration.

The amount of effort involved with dehydrating and rehydrating server controls can be significant, especially if the information is of a large size. In most cases, the amount of work involved is not much smaller than binding the controls to a data source.

To prove our point, we will create a Web page that runs several SQL statements on the Northwind database and uses their results to populate a number of drop-down lists and a data grid control. The results from the SQL statements are later cached by using a DataSet object.

We will then create an Application Center test script that conducts performance tests on this Web page by using two scenarios. In one scenario, we will enable view state for all controls and not rebind the controls with the cached data set. In the second scenario, we will disable view state for all drop-down lists and the data grid control and use the cached DataSet object to rebind to these controls. You will see that the Web page worked with almost identical performance in both scenarios.

Listing 2-10 shows the code for a Web page that contains several drop-down lists and a data grid control. These controls are populated from the Northwind database.

Listing 2-10. Web Page Containing Various Data-Bound Controls

```
private void Page_Load(object sender, System.EventArgs e)
{
    // To bind controls to data source on every request,
    // simply comment the following conditional statement.
    if (!IsPostBack)
    {
        DataSet MyDataSet;
```

```
// If cache is empty, run SQL and generate DataSet from
// the database.
if (Cache["Orders"] == null)
{
    MyDataSet = new DataSet();
    SqlDataAdapter MyAdapter = new SqlDataAdapter();

    SqlCommand MyCommand = new SqlCommand();
    MyCommand.Connection = new SqlConnection("Connection String");
    MyAdapter.SelectCommand = MyCommand;

    MyCommand.Connection.Open();

    // Creating six data tables. They will be used to
    // bind to drop-down lists.
    MyCommand.CommandText = " SELECT * FROM Categories ";
    MyAdapter.Fill(MyDataSet, "Categories");

    MyCommand.CommandText = " SELECT * FROM Customers ";
    MyAdapter.Fill(MyDataSet, "Customers");

    MyCommand.CommandText = " SELECT * FROM Employees ";
    MyAdapter.Fill(MyDataSet, "Employees");

    MyCommand.CommandText = " SELECT * FROM Orders ";
    MyAdapter.Fill(MyDataSet, "Orders");

    MyCommand.CommandText = " SELECT * FROM Products ";
    MyAdapter.Fill(MyDataSet, "Products");

    MyCommand.CommandText = " SELECT * FROM Region ";
    MyAdapter.Fill(MyDataSet, "Region");


    // Filling the data grid with order summary. This
    // SQL statement returns 72 records.
    MyCommand.CommandText = " select Orders.OrderID," +
    " Customers.CompanyName, Employees.LastName," +
    " Employees.FirstName, Orders.OrderDate," +
    " Orders.RequiredDate, Orders.ShippedDate" +
    " from Orders, Customers, Employees" +
    " where Orders.CustomerID = Customers.CustomerID" +
    " and Orders.EmployeeID = Employees.EmployeeID" +
    " and Employees.LastName = 'King' ";
```

```
                    MyAdapter.Fill(MyDataSet, "OrderList");

                    MyCommand.Connection.Close();
                    MyCommand.Connection.Dispose();
                    MyCommand.Dispose();

                    // Adding newly created data set to cache.
                    Cache["Orders"] = MyDataSet;
            }
            else
            {

                    // Because cache is not empty, retrieving the data set
                    // from it.
                    MyDataSet = Cache["Orders"] as DataSet;

            }


                    // Binding the data set to all six drop-down lists and
                    // the data grid control.
                    CategoriesDropDown.DataSource =
                          MyDataSet.Tables["Categories"].DefaultView;
                    CustomersDropDown.DataSource =
                          MyDataSet.Tables["Customers"].DefaultView;
                    EmployeesDropDown.DataSource =
                          MyDataSet.Tables["Employees"].DefaultView;
                    OrdersDropDown.DataSource =
                        MyDataSet.Tables["Orders"].DefaultView;
                    ProductsDropDown.DataSource =
                        MyDataSet.Tables["Products"].DefaultView;
                    RegionDropDown.DataSource =
                        MyDataSet.Tables["Region"].DefaultView;
                    ResultGrid.DataSource =
                        MyDataSet.Tables["OrderList"].DefaultView;

                    CategoriesDropDown.DataBind();
                    CustomersDropDown.DataBind();
                    EmployeesDropDown.DataBind();
                    OrdersDropDown.DataBind();
                    ProductsDropDown.DataBind();
                    RegionDropDown.DataBind();
                    ResultGrid.DataBind();
            }
        }
```

When you compile and run the code shown in Listing 2-10, you will see the Web page shown in Figure 2-8.

| Post Back |

Categories: Beverages
Customers: Alfreds Futterkiste
Employees: Davolio

Orders: 7/4/1996 12:00:00 AM
Products: Chai
Region: Eastern

OrderID	CompanyName	LastName	FirstName	OrderDate
10289	B's Beverages	King	Robert	8/26/1996 12:00:00 AM
10303	Godos Cocina Típica	King	Robert	9/11/1996 12:00:00 AM
10308	Ana Trujillo Emparedados y helados	King	Robert	9/18/1996 12:00:00 AM
10319	Tortuga Restaurante	King	Robert	10/2/1996 12:00:00 AM
10322	Pericles Comidas clásicas	King	Robert	10/4/1996 12:00:00 AM
10335	Hungry Owl All-Night Grocers	King	Robert	10/22/1996 12:00:00 AM
10336	Princesa Isabel Vinhos	King	Robert	10/23/1996 12:00:00 AM
10341	Simons bistro	King	Robert	10/29/1996 12:00:00 AM
10349	Split Rail Beer & Ale	King	Robert	11/8/1996 12:00:00 AM
10353	Piccolo und mehr	King	Robert	11/13/1996 12:00:00 AM
10367	Vaffeljernet	King	Robert	11/28/1996 12:00:00 AM
10406	Queen Cozinha	King	Robert	1/7/1997 12:00:00 AM
10424	Mère Paillarde	King	Robert	1/23/1997 12:00:00 AM

Figure 2-8. A partial snapshot of the Web page contains information from the Northwind database

Clicking the Post Back button resubmits the page. We deliberately didn't write any code in the event handler for the button because we didn't want to incur any overhead during post-back, other than the maintenance of view state for the server controls.

Now that you have seen the code and the user interface for this Web page, let us show you the results from the performance tests we conducted, as shown in Figure 2-9. As promised, we conducted the performance test with and without enabling view state for all drop-down lists and the data grid control.

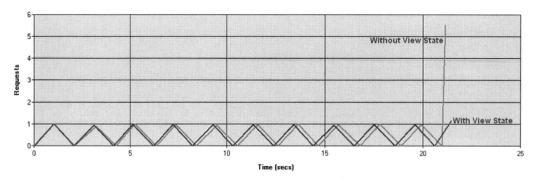

Figure 2-9. The result of Application Center performance test with and without using view state

There you have it! There is not much difference in performance whether you use view state to maintain information during post-back or rebind your server controls to a data source on each post-back. The only assumption made is that you must cache the data source to get comparable performance.

Understanding the Session Object

As you know, the Session object enables you to maintain user-specific information in memory cache. The ASP.NET runtime automatically creates this object when a new user visits your Web site, and it remains in memory for a specific period after the user stops using the Web site. You can alter the duration for which the Session object remains in memory by changing the session timeout setting in the Web.config file. The timeout is set to 20 minutes by default.

In this section, we will show you the impact on performance for different session configurations. The ASP.NET framework enables us to store session state either in Web server memory, in a Windows service, or in a SQL Server database. Each of you has to decide the configuration that best suits your environment. We will attempt to provide enough information to make this selection easy for you. You should remember that session configuration is simply the matter of setting a few switches in the Web.config file and therefore you can change them any time you feel a need to reconfigure your mechanism for maintaining session state.

In-Process Session

The default session state setting is InProc. When configured with this setting, the ASP.NET runtime keeps all session information in the Web application's memory. Because the session is stored in the application's memory, it is much faster to get the stored information. On the other hand, if your Web application restarts for any reason, you will lose every object stored in every user's session. You need to choose whether this is an acceptable compromise in your situation. Keeping session "in-process" also prohibits you from scaling your Web applications by using a *server farm*, which consists of multiple Web servers working in tandem. The incoming requests for Web pages are automatically routed to the least busy server in the farm. In this scenario, the in-process session is not a viable option as Web servers in the farm are unable to read each other's in-process memory.

State Server

The ASP.NET framework enables us to store session information by using a Windows service. Because the Windows service runs as an independent process, information stored in the service is not affected when the Web application is restarted. Also, other Web servers in the server farm can communicate with the Windows service to get access to the session information stored in it.

The bottom line is that the state server enables us to scale our Web application by using a server farm. It is also more robust than an in-process session because it does not depend on the Web application's memory. You can restart your Web application or Web server as many times as you please without losing session information. Rebooting the server, on the other hand, will cause you to lose the session information. If you are paranoid about losing session information during an unplanned server reboot, you need to use the database-enabled session instead.

SQL Server Session

We also have the ability to store session information in a SQL Server 7.0 or later database. This option also allows us to scale our Web site in the server farm environment because all servers in the farm can access the same SQL Server database. Common sense tells us that this option would demand the heaviest performance penalty, but you are about to discover that it isn't necessary so. The database-based session management may lose the performance battle if your

Web site handles hundreds of concurrent users. Otherwise, its performance is quite comparable to the state server.

However, you do get other benefits by not using your SQL Server database for session management. At the least, it keeps the database available for more business-critical processing. The choice between state server and the SQL Server state management needs to be made individually for each project. Depending on the application's needs, either choice could be the right choice for you.

 BEST PRACTICE *The state server option can out-perform in the heaviest traffic area, but it allows you to keep your database resource available for critical business transactions, such as order processing, credit checking, reporting, etc. The SQL Server state management option allows you to maintain session information robustly, allowing for session recovery after a server reboot. On the other hand, it demands heavy use of your most valuable resource, the database server.*

Performance Testing the Session Object

It is more fun to see the Session object in action than just to talk about it. We conducted a series of performance tests on various session configurations and saw the results in this chapter. We conducted all tests by using the Application Center test and simulated 10 simultaneous Web users.

The tests are divided into two categories. The small session tests use the Session object to store a small piece of information, no more than a few characters. The large session tests store a data set that contains 100 rows retrieved from the Orders table of the Northwind database.

Each of these categories contains tests performed by using a combination of in-process, state server, and SQL Server settings. In the case of state server and SQL Server settings, tests were conducted by keeping the session on the same server as the Web site and on a remote server. Figure 2-10 shows performance from using the in-process session while session contains a small amount of information.

You can clearly see that the Web site was able to serve about 235 requests per second. The occasional drop in performance can be attributed to external influences generated by other applications running on the same server. On the average, the Web site was about able to serve more than 200 requests consistently.

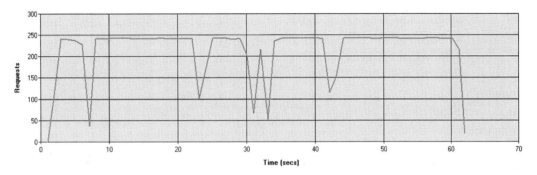

Figure 2-10. Performance using the in-process session containing a small amount of information

Figure 2-11 shows performance from using the state server session containing a small amount of information. The test was conducted in two scenarios. In one scenario, the Web server was used as state server, and in the second scenario, the state server was used on a remote computer.

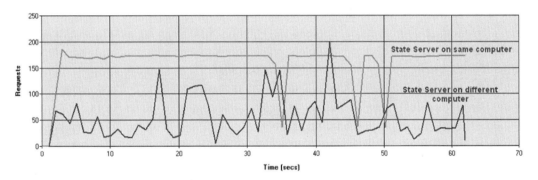

Figure 2-11. Performance using the state server

As you probably expected, the Web site performed better when the same computer that hosted the Web site was used for state server. The performance drops quite significantly when you host the state server on a remote computer. In either case, the performance is quite a bit slower than keeping in-process session.

Now that we have seen the performance from using in-process and state server options, let us show you the performance results from using SQL Server for state management. There are those who like to tell everyone that using a relational database engine for anything results in slower performance than storing the same content in memory. This theory used to be true years ago when the relational database engines were in their infancy. However, the newer versions of such systems are quite fast and can handle a much greater load than before. But why should you take our word? See for yourself!

Figure 2-12 shows performance from using a SQL Server session that contains a small amount of information. The test was conducted in two scenarios. In one scenario, the Web server was used for SQL Server state management, and in the second scenario, the SQL Server was used on a remote computer.

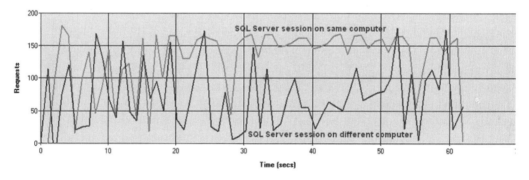

Figure 2-12. Performance using the SQL Server

Surprising, isn't it? Storing session information in a SQL Server database on the same computer provided comparable performance to the state server option. On the other hand, using the SQL Server database on a remote computer provided slightly better performance than using state server on a remote computer. The only strange thing about using SQL Server is that it seems to be quite erratic. The performance seems to change quite drastically from one request to another. We can't explain this phenomenon. Perhaps someone more knowledgeable about SQL Server can shed some light.

Table 2-2 summarizes the test results. Remember, these tests are conducted with a small amount of information in session. The performance slows down significantly as you start to put larger amounts of content in session.

Table 2-2. Performance Results from Using Various Session Configurations

SESSION TYPE	AVERAGE PERFORMANCE	EXPLANATION
In-Process	235 requests/second	Provides the fastest performance because it doesn't have the overhead of out-process marshalling.
State Server, Same Computer	170 requests/second	Provides 30 percent slower performance than the in-process session. However, the content stored in session is not lost when the Web application restarts.
State Server, Different Computer	55 requests/second	There is about 68 percent decrease in performance if you choose to use a remote server as state server. If you are building a Web application for a server farm, you have no choice but to use a remote server for session management. Otherwise, you won't be able to share the same session information across all servers in the farm.

Performance Testing Session with a Large Amount of Content

All our tests so far have used a small amount of content in the Session object. The session performance starts to decline significantly as we put larger amounts of content in it. The change in performance seems to affect only the state server and the SQL Server session management options. We found that the in-process session didn't show any effect on performance, whether we kept small or large quantities of information in it.

The next set of test results show the drastic decline in performance when we put a DataSet object that contains 100 rows from the Orders table of the Northwind database.

Figure 2-13 shows performance from using the SQL Server and state server options. Both options were used while keeping session on the same computer as the Web site. The Session object contained a large quantity of information.

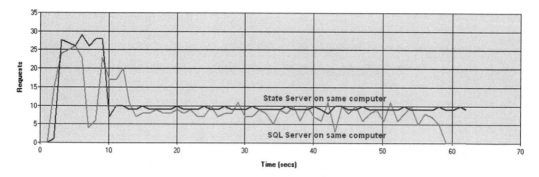

Figure 2-13. Performance using SQL Server and state server

Were we right, or were we right? Actually, we are quite surprised to see such a drastic decline in performance. The slow down is attributed to the fact that the large quantity of information needs to be sent across the process boundary. Regardless of the reason, it is quite amazing to see that the performance declined from 160 requests per second to a meager nine requests per second simply because we chose to store 100 records from the database. Keep this statistic in mind next time you choose to put a large quantity of data in session and still want to use the state server or SQL Server session option.

We repeated the same performance tests, keeping the state server and SQL server on a remote computer. As expected, the performance declined even further, averaging about six requests per second.

Someone Call the Session Doctor!

You will be quite surprised to learn that the decline in session performance with a large quantity of information is the result of a very common mistake. It's a mistake most of us make and never even realize its consequences. Even though the solution is very simple, we are willing to bet a dime that more than 90 percent of the readers of this book either don't know this solution or don't use it on a regular basis.

The solution is to use the ReadOnly session wherever possible. Most Web applications store information in session so that they can be accessed at a later time on a different Web page. We don't always need to modify this information. Often, we simply need to access it. Take our advice and use the following keyword in the @Page directive of every page that only needs read-only access to the session.

```
EnableSessionState=ReadOnly
```

This is it! This is all you need to do to increase the performance by at least 10 times. Figure 2-14 shows performance with the state server ReadOnly session containing a large quantity of information. The state server uses the same computer as the Web server.

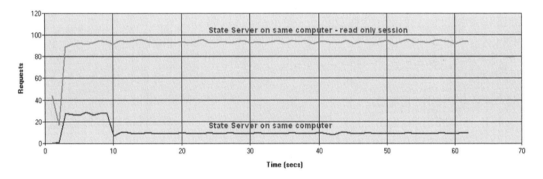

Figure 2-14. Performance using the ReadOnly session

The performance increases sharply during read-only access to session because the ASP.NET runtime doesn't attempt to persist the session information back to its original location when the page finishes rendering, resulting in fewer marshalling calls across process boundaries.

Summary

In this chapter, you learned the facts behind keeping information in server memory. It can be a rewarding experience, providing enormous performance and scalability gains. On the other hand, if used improperly, it can cost your application its performance and precious memory resources. Our intention was to show you the realities behind various cache, session, and view state options, hoping that you will use these features to their full capabilities.

CHAPTER 3

Client-Side JavaScript: Oh, What Fun!

WE HAVE PROBABLY READ just about every book written on ASP.NET. Some are good, detail-oriented books while some others are merely introductory books that only touch key topics on the surface. Regardless of the level of depth these books provide, most of them don't educate readers on ways of writing client-side JavaScript.

Though these books cover lots of information on ASP.NET, they don't give a straightforward guide on how to check for a valid input value. You don't necessarily want to make a round trip to the server and take that hefty performance penalty just to check for a valid input value; you can do that on the client in a few milliseconds. We have had the JavaScript versus post-back conversation at least a dozen times with a variety of developers from a wide range of industries. Being consultants enables us to work with a diverse range of clients, helping them understand the impact of the ASP.NET technology. Soon after we get into the details of the post-back mechanism, some insightful programmer in the room always questions how ASP.NET supports JavaScript.

It's time to start educating programmers on how effectively to use JavaScript with the ASP.NET post-back mechanism to provide an efficient and reliable experience to the users of our Web applications. Even the creators of ASP.NET know this. The validation controls that ship with the framework make good use of client-side JavaScript to validate user input without having to make a round trip to the server.

We believe that every project team needs to decide on the amount of JavaScript they want to develop and support. JavaScript is not necessarily an easy language to work with. It provides virtually no support for advance debugging. It may behave differently on different browsers and on different versions of the same browser. When your project team decides to develop parts of the application by using JavaScript, it needs to be mentally and technically prepared to deal with its implications.

JavaScript can not only boost the application performance but can also provide a seamless and efficient experience to the users, specially those who use a slow Internet connection to browse your Web site.

For example, suppose you are asked to provide a drop-down list of credit card numbers, and, when the user selects a number, to display the cardholder name and expiration date by using text boxes. One way to accomplish this task is to capture the SelectedIndexChange event of the ASP.NET drop-down list control. When this event occurs, the page makes a post-back trip to the server and triggers your event handler. In the event handler, you can obtain the selected credit card number and retrieve remaining information by querying the database. This mechanism, even though it is an ASP.NET way of accomplishing tasks, is very slow and causes unnecessary traffic on the Web server.

This chapter shows an alternative approach to server-side event processing. It focuses on showing various aspects of using JavaScript with ASP.NET code to provide a rich and seamless user experience. When you are done reading this chapter, you will be able to create a JavaScript array dynamically and call a JavaScript function when the user selects an item from the list. By using this function, you can retrieve remaining information by searching the array. The JavaScript approach will be extremely fast and will not create an unnecessary load on the Web server.

Capturing Events Raised by HTML Controls with JavaScript

A significant feature of the JavaScript language is its ability to capture events fired by HTML controls that reside on the page. Notice that we used the term HTML controls instead of Web controls. Web controls are ASP.NET server controls that exist only on the Web server and perform all their functions while residing on the server. They are not available to the JavaScript code that runs in the browser and works on the HTML received from the Web server.

Prior to ASP.NET, receiving events from HTML controls was quite simple. Because Web controls didn't exist, the Web server directly manipulated HTML tags. In the past, when we needed to capture such event, we would simply use the JavaScript syntax for capturing such events and provide either inline JavaScript code or call a JavaScript function. The following example shows how events are captured in JavaScript:

```
<input type="button" value="Hello" id="MyButton"
onClick="javascript:alert('Hi')">
```

When you place the preceding line of code in any HTML page, you will see a button with the text "Hello" on it. When you click this button, a JavaScript alert box that says "Hi" will appear. Accomplishing this task in ASP.NET is not as simple as it probably should be. If you need to create a button control in ASP.NET, chances are that you want a Web server control so that you can still capture post-back events and perform tasks on the Web server. In addition, if you also want to capture a client-side event by using JavaScript, you can't simply use the onClick syntax as we did in the preceding example. The Web control considers onClick as the server-side event and will perform a post-back operation.

```
<asp:Button ID="AlsoMyButton" Runat=server Text="Hi"
onClick="javascript:alert('Hi')"></asp:Button>
```

If you place the preceding line of code in an ASP.NET page, you will get an error message when you try to access the page. You'll get this error message, which says that JavaScript is not a member of your Web page, because <asp:Button> represents a Web server control and the onClick attribute of this tag must refer to a server-side event handler and not to JavaScript code. The proper way of using the mentioned server control is shown here:

```
<asp:Button ID="AlsoMyButton" Runat=server Text="Hi"
onClick="DoSomethingOnServer"></asp:Button>
```

As you can see, the onClick event is wired with the DoSomethingOnServer event handler, which is simply a method you should provide, preferably in code behind, for server-side execution. Following is an example of such server-side event handler:

```
Public Sub DoSomethingOnServer(ByVal sender As System.Object, _
         ByVal e As System.EventArgs)

    ' Server-side code.
End Sub
```

So how can you wire client-side JavaScript event handlers by using the Web server controls? Unfortunately, there is no easy way to do it. In fact, the only way for you to capture a client-side event is to add an attribute to the server control.

Server Control Attributes

An *attribute* is a name-value pair that is appended to the HTML tag rendered by the server control. For example, the <asp:Button> server control renders the <Input type="Submit"> HTML tag. If you want to add a JavaScript event handler, you need to add an attribute to this tag. The attribute name should be the event name, such as onClick, and the attribute value should be the JavaScript code you want to execute. Listing 3-1 shows how to add an onClick JavaScript event handler to a <asp:Button> server control.

Listing 3-1. Capturing the JavaScript Event by Using a Server Control

```
Private Sub Page_Load(ByVal sender As System.Object, _
                       ByVal e As System.EventArgs) Handles MyBase.Load

    If Not IsPostBack Then
        MyButton.Attributes.Add("onClick ", "javascript:alert('Hi')")
    End If
End Sub
```

In this example, we used the Add method of the Attributes collection to add the JavaScript event handler. Every server control has the Attributes collection, whose purpose is to provide us with the ability to add custom attributes to the rendered HTML tag. When you compile and execute the preceding code shown, the rendered HTML looks like this:

```
<input type="submit" name="MyButton" value="Hello" id="MyButton"
onClick="javascript:alert('Hi')" />
```

You can clearly see that we effectively added the onClick JavaScript handler by using the Attributes collection. Needless to say, it was easier to do so before ASP.NET, when we didn't have to manage JavaScript code and event handlers programmatically.

JavaScript in ASP.NET: A Problematic Solution

The problem with the ASP.NET mechanism for managing JavaScript is that it forces us to generate JavaScript from the code. Previously, we were able simply to write JavaScript in the HTML file and make changes to it as needed. Now, because we are generating it from our server-side code, every change to the JavaScript causes us to recompile and redeploy our application. To make matters worse, we are also forced to write JavaScript code in a String variable. Imagine multiple lines of JavaScript code written in a single String variable. You wouldn't want to be the one to write or debug that code.

 NOTE *It's a grim situation. Programmers risk creating unmanageable JavaScript code. Perhaps it's a sacrifice we all have to make to please the gods of ASP.NET, who blessed us with programmable server controls, post-back event processing, code behind, and other such amenities and in return demand that we sacrifice our ability to write elaborate client-side code. Perhaps we are being a tad dramatic; nonetheless, the fact remains that we need to learn a different way of programming with JavaScript.*

We can avoid many problems by choosing not to hard-code any JavaScript code in Web pages. It has always been a best practice to write all the JavaScript code in the form of reusable functions and store them in a .js file. However, many programmers didn't follow these guidelines and wrote dozens of lines of inline code and mixed it up with HTML tags. The syntax you need to use to link an ASP.NET page with a JavaScript source file (.js) is shown here:

```
<script language="javascript" src="/includes/JavaScriptSourceFile.js"></script>
```

 BEST PRACTICE *We can't stress enough that the need has never been greater for managing client-side scripts in the form of reusable functions and preferably storing them in a .js file. If we don't become organized and start treating client-side script as a key reusable code component, we will soon find ourselves battling the intricacies of ASP.NET to execute even the simplest client-side script.*

Luckily, the mechanism for writing a JavaScript code block hasn't changed in ASP.NET. We can still use the <script language=javascript> block to store JavaScript code.

Dynamically Generating JavaScript Code

ASP.NET provides us with the capability of dynamically generating a JavaScript code block, which is a very powerful feature that can provide many benefits but also comes with its own risks. This section shows ways in which to use these features to our advantage and to avoid falling into traps. The Page class, the base class for all ASP.NET pages, provides a number of methods for generating client-side script. Table 3-1 lists these methods and their intended purposes. We discuss each method in more detail in the sections that follow.

Table 3-1. Methods for Dynamically Generating Client-Side JavaScript Code

METHOD NAME	PARAMETERS	EXPLANATION
RegisterArrayDeclaration	Array Name, Array Value	This method generates a JavaScript array declaration by using the name and the values you provide. It is very useful for prepopulating a list of values from the server when the page is loaded. You can later use JavaScript to process these values.
RegisterClientScriptBlock	Key, Script	Use this method to generate a <Script> block that contains JavaScript code. You will have to provide complete JavaScript code, including the <Script> and </Script> tags. You can assign a name to this code block by using a key parameter that can later be used to retrieve the code block programmatically.
RegisterOnSubmitStatement	Key, Script	Use this method to generate JavaScript code that will execute when the form is submitted. You can either provide inline JavaScript code or call a predefined JavaScript function.
RegisterStartupScript	Key, Script	Use this method to generate JavaScript code that will execute when the page is loaded in the browser. You can either provide inline JavaScript code or call a predefined JavaScript function.

BEST PRACTICE *If you are using Visual Basic .NET, you may not see any of the previously mentioned JavaScript handler methods in the IntelliSense. This behavior happens because the Visual Basic .NET environment hides advance methods from the programmers. (Go figure! The Visual Basic .NET cult should protest against discrimination.)*

To view advance methods, choose Options from the Tools menu in Visual Studio .NET. From the Options dialog box, open the Text Editor folder and select Basic. Make sure to clear the Hide Advance Members check box.

Using the RegisterArrayDeclaration Method

You might often need to enhance the user experience by using a JavaScript array that needs to be populated by values from the database. Creating an array for JavaScript use can minimize the number of trips back to the Web server, which not only reduces the amount of traffic on the server but also simultaneously provides a rich user interface.

Such logic can be applicable in various scenarios. If you are creating an eCommerce site, you might need to display a list of product variations. Many eCommerce applications are capable of showing the same product in various colors, sizes, and designs. Each combination often has its own image that needs to be displayed as the user flips through the choices. You can provide this feature by using the traditional approach of submitting the page every time the user makes a selection, or you can prepopulate a JavaScript array with the desired information and use it in client-side JavaScript code to provide a seamless user experience.

Let's create a simple Web page to demonstrate the RegisterArrayDeclaration method. This page provides a slide show where the client-side JavaScript changes the image. In this example, we will search a specified folder on the server and load the names of all the images in a JavaScript array. We will also provide two buttons, one for showing the next image from the list and another for showing the previous one.

Figure 3-1 shows three pictures because the folder that was used to load images only contained these three images. The beauty of this code is that you can completely customize as many images as you want to preload in the JavaScript array. Once the page is loaded in the browser, it doesn't need to submit back to the server just to change the image. The code in Listing 3-2 shows how you can switch images at the click of the button by using a preloaded JavaScript array.

Figure 3-1. The slide show Web page. You can see the images that were loaded from the Images folder on the Web server.

Listing 3-2. JavaScript Code for Changing the Image When the Back or Next Buttons Are Clicked

```
<SCRIPT language=javascript>
    var curPic = 0;

    function processPrevious()
    {
        if (curPic==0)
        {
            curPic=Pictures.length - 1;
        }
        else
        {
            curPic--;
        }
        document.myPicture.src=Pictures[curPic];
    }

    function processNext()
    {
        if (curPic==Pictures.length -1)
        {
            curPic=0;
        }
        else
        {
            curPic++;
        }
        document.myPicture.src=Pictures[curPic];
    }
</SCRIPT>
```

You can see in this JavaScript code that it uses the Pictures array to retrieve the name of the picture it needs to show. This array is not defined anywhere in the .js file or in the Web page. Instead, our ASP.NET server-side code will dynamically generate this array when the page is rendered. In Listing 3-3, we will write a few lines of server-side ASP.NET code by using Visual Basic .NET to get a list of all the images stored in a specific folder. Using this list of images, we will proceed with dynamically generating a JavaScript array that contains paths to these images. The beauty of this mechanism is that the JavaScript array is completely dynamic and will automatically pick up new images as you drop them in the right folder.

The processNext method checks to see if the current picture is the last in the list. If it is, it shows the first picture from the list. If it is not, it shows the next picture from the list. The processPrevious method checks to see if the current picture is the first picture in the list. If it is, it shows the last picture from the list. If it is not, it shows the previous picture from the list.

Listing 3-3. ASP.NET Code for Dynamically Creating and Populating a JavaScript Array

```
Private Sub Page_Load(ByVal sender As System.Object, _
        ByVal e As System.EventArgs) Handles MyBase.Load

    If Not Page.IsPostBack Then
        Dim ImageArray As StringBuilder

            ' The GetImageArray method searches the Images
            ' folder and returns a JavaScript array declaration
            ' for all files contained in the folder.
            ImageArray = GetImageArray("Images")

            ' Once we have the array declaration, we simply add it
            ' to the page by using the RegisterArrayDeclaration method.
            ' The name of the JavaScript array will be Pictures,
            ' as specified in the first parameter.
            Page.RegisterArrayDeclaration("Pictures", ImageArray.ToString())

            ' Wiring the Back button's click event to
            ' the processPrevious function. Make sure to
                ' return false in order to disable post-back operation.
                BackButton.Attributes.Add("onClick", "processPrevious();return
false;")

                    ' Wiring the Next button's click event to
                    ' the processNext function. Make sure to
                    ' return false in order to disable post-back operation.
                    NextButton.Attributes.Add("onClick", "processNext();return false;")
        End If
    End Sub

    ' This function receives a folder name and returns a
    ' JavaScript array declaration containing names of all files
    ' from the folder.
    Private Function GetImageArray(ByVal folderName As String)  As
StringBuilder
```

```
            Dim Path As String
            Dim Folder As DirectoryInfo
            Dim Image As FileInfo
            Dim Images As FileInfo()
            Dim ImageArray As New StringBuilder()

            Path = Request.PhysicalApplicationPath + folderName
            Folder = New DirectoryInfo(Path)
            Images = Folder.GetFiles()

            ' Looping through all files in the folder and generating
            ' a JavaScript array declaration.
            For Each Image In Images
                ImageArray.AppendFormat("'{0}/{1}',", folderName, Image.Name)
            Next

            ' Removing the unwanted last comma.
            ImageArray.Remove(ImageArray.Length - 1, 1)

            Return ImageArray
        End Function
```

The HTML page generated by this example is shown in Listing 3-4. For the sake of clarity, we have included the JavaScript functions in the HTML file, but you should remember from our previous discussion that you should always try to keep all such functions in a .js file.

Listing 3-4. HTML Page Generated from the Slide Show Example

```
<HTML>
<HEAD>
    <title>JavaScript Array</title>

    <!-- JavaScript functions for changing the image. -- >
    <SCRIPT language=javascript>
        var curPic = 0;

        function processPrevious()
        {
        if (curPic==0)
        {
            curPic=Pictures.length - 1;
        }
```

```
        else
        {
            curPic--;
        }
        document.myPicture.src=Pictures[curPic];
    }


    function processNext()
    {
        if (curPic==Pictures.length -1)
        {
            curPic=0;
        }
        else
        {
            curPic++;
        }
        document.myPicture.src=Pictures[curPic];
    }


    </SCRIPT>
    </HEAD>


    <body>
        <form name="Form1" method="post" action="JavaScriptArray.aspx"
id="Form1">


            <input type="hidden" name="__VIEWSTATE"
                value="dDwtMTE5MjkxMzIxODs7PhR4ev3gXAGrPsQB8W8p1TDusx61" />


            <img id="myPicture" name="myPicture" src="/ASPNETVB/images/ac1.jpg"/>


            <!-- The Next button handles onClick JavaScript event. -- >
            <input type="submit" name="BackButton" value="Back" id="BackButton"
                        onClick="processPrevious();return false;"/>


            <!-- The Back button handles onClick JavaScript event. -- >
            <input type="submit" name="NextButton" value="Next" id="NextButton"
                        onClick="processNext();return false;"/>


            <!-- The RegisterArrayDeclaration method added the following script
            block. You can clearly see the array declaration containing names of
            the files we generated programmatically. -- >
```

```
        <script language="javascript">
            <!--
                    var Pictures =  new
Array('Images/ac1.jpg','Images/ac2.jpg','Images/ac3.jpg');
                // -->
        </script>
        </form>
    </body>
</HTML>
```

Using the RegisterClientScriptBlock Method

This method allows us to generate JavaScript code dynamically and place it on the page. It also allows us to remove a previously placed JavaScript method from the page. This method comes in very handy if you write server controls that generate JavaScript. Using this method from within the server control ensures that the JavaScript is generated only once, which helps remove the redundancy when you use more than one instance of the server control in a Web page.

The problem with this method is that it wants us to provide the entire JavaScript code block in one String variable. Imagine writing the previously mentioned processNext and processPrevious methods in one line! Better yet, let's try to see how it looks (see Listing 3-5).

Listing 3-5. Injecting JavaScript Methods by Using Server-Side Code

```
Private Sub Page_Load(ByVal sender As System.Object, _
        ByVal e As System.EventArgs) Handles MyBase.Load

    If Not Page.IsPostBack Then

        Dim CurPic As String
        Dim ProcessPrevious, ProcessNext As String

        CurPic = "var curPic = 0;"

            ' Programmatically generating processPrevious function.
        ProcessPrevious = "function processPrevious() " + _
            " { " + _
            "   if (curPic==0) " + _
            "   { " + _
            "     curPic=Pictures.length - 1; " + _
            "   } " + _
```

```
         "  else " + _
         "  { " + _
         "    curPic--; " + _
         "  } " + _
         "  document.myPicture.src=Pictures[curPic]; " + _
         " } "

    ' Programmatically generating processNext function.
ProcessNext = "function processNext() " + _
         " { " + _
         "    if (curPic==Pictures.length -1) " + _
         "    { " + _
         "       curPic=0; " + _
         "    } " + _
         "    else " + _
         "    { " + _
         "       curPic++; " + _
         "    } " + _
         "    document.myPicture.src=Pictures[curPic];" + _
         " }"

    ' Calling the  RegisterClientScriptBlock method to generate
    ' processNext and processPrevious JavaScript functions.
    ' Remember to use the <script> and </script> tags, or the
    ' method will not generate these scripts for you.

    Page.RegisterClientScriptBlock("SlideShow", _
            "<script language='JavaScript'>" + _
            CurPic + ProcessPrevious + ProcessNext + _
            "</script>")

    BackButton.Attributes.Add("onClick", _
        "processPrevious();return false;")
    NextButton.Attributes.Add("onClick",
        "processNext();return false;")

  myPicture.Attributes.Add("onMouseOver", "processNext()")

  End If
End Sub
```

The resulting HTML is shown in Listing 3-6.

Listing 3-6. The JavaScript Generated by the RegisterClientScriptBlock Method

```
<HTML>
    <HEAD>
        <title>Register Client Script Block Test</title>
    </HEAD>

    <body>
        <form name="Form1" method="post"
            action="JavaScriptCodeBlock.aspx" id="Form1">
        <input type="hidden" name="__VIEWSTATE"
            value="dDwtMTE5MjkxMzIxODs7PpB6ZOAgG+eKyRO46Uvl83R75GCj" />

<!-- Following is the script generated by RegisterClientScriptBlock method.
    It is hard to read and even harder to maintain. -- >
<script language='JavaScript'>var curPic = 0;function processPrevious()
{ if (curPic==0)   {     curPic=Pictures.length - 1;   }
else  {     curPic--;   } document.myPicture.src=Pictures[curPic];   }
    function processNext()  {  if  (curPic==Pictures.length -1)
    { curPic=0; }  else {  curPic++; }
    document.myPicture.src=Pictures[curPic];   }</script>

        <!-- Image control. -- >
        <img id="myPicture" name="myPicture" src="/ASPNETVB/images/ac1.jpg" />

        <!-- Back button. -- >
        <input type="submit" name="BackButton" value="Back" id="BackButton"
            onClick="processPrevious();return false;"/>

        <!-- Next button. -- >
        <input type="submit" name="NextButton" value="Next" id="NextButton"
            onClick="processNext();return false;" />

        <!-- Auto-generated JavaScript array. -- >
        <script language="javascript">
<!--
var Pictures =  new Array('Images/ac1.jpg','Images/ac2.jpg','Images/ac3.jpg');
// -->
        </script>
        </form>
    </body>
</HTML>
```

CAUTION *Needless to say, this style of programming is looking to get you in trouble. Sooner or later, you will be asked to make changes to the JavaScript code and, it won't be long before you start banging your head on your cube walls, calling names at the people who allowed you to write JavaScript in this fashion.*

If you have a dying need to auto-generate snippets of JavaScript code and you simply can't store them in the reusable .js file, we recommend that you store this JavaScript code in a text file on the server and read its content by using the classes defined in the System.IO namespace. At the least, the JavaScript code won't be hard-coded in your code behind and it will be much easier to maintain this code at a later time.

Using the RegisterStartupScript Method

You can use this method to process JavaScript code when the page is loaded in the browser. It also suffers from the same problems as the RegisterClientScriptBlock method because it also requires us to provide JavaScript code contained in a String variable.

It is best to use this method either to provide a very short JavaScript code or to call a JavaScript method contained in the .js file. The following example shows how to use this method and the resulting HTML. Also, use this method only if you need to inject startup code selectively. If your startup code never changes, it is best simply to hard-code it in the .aspx page itself. Listing 3-7 shows server-side code for registering a startup JavaScript code.

Listing 3-7. Server-Side Code for Registering a Startup JavaScript Code

```
Private Sub Page_Load(ByVal sender As System.Object, _
        ByVal e As System.EventArgs) Handles MyBase.Load

  If Not Page.IsPostBack Then

  Dim ImageArray As StringBuilder

  ImageArray = GetImageArray("Images")
  Page.RegisterArrayDeclaration("Pictures", ImageArray.ToString())
  BackButton.Attributes.Add("onClick", "processPrevious();return false;")
  NextButton.Attributes.Add("onClick", "processNext();return false;")
```

```
        myPicture.Attributes.Add("onMouseOver", "processNext()")

    ' Registering startup script. This script displays a
    ' message box saying "Hi" then calls the processNext
    ' method. Remember to use the <script> and </script> tags.
    Page.RegisterStartupScript("StartUp", _
        "<script language='JavaScript'>alert('Hi');processNext()</script>")

    End If
End Sub

Private Function GetImageArray(ByVal folderName As String) As StringBuilder
    Dim Path As String
    Dim Folder As DirectoryInfo
    Dim Image As FileInfo
    Dim Images As FileInfo()
    Dim ImageArray As New StringBuilder()

    Path = Request.PhysicalApplicationPath + folderName
    Folder = New DirectoryInfo(Path)
    Images = Folder.GetFiles()

    For Each Image In Images
        ImageArray.AppendFormat("'{0}/{1}',", folderName, Image.Name)
    Next
    ImageArray.Remove(ImageArray.Length - 1, 1)

    Return ImageArray
End Function
```

The resulting HTML is shown in Listing 3-8. You will see that there is nothing exciting about this HTML. The RegisterStartupScript method simply takes the input string and writes it in the middle of the page. We could have written this content using the Response.Write method.

Listing 3-8. JavaScript Generated by Using the RegisterStartupScript Method

```
<HTML>
  <HEAD>
  <title>JavascriptArray</title>
    <SCRIPT language=Javascript>
     var curPic = 0;
       function processPrevious() {
```

```
      if (curPic==0)
      {
        curPic=Pictures.length - 1;
      }
      else
      {
        curPic--;
      }
      document.myPicture.src=Pictures[curPic];
  }

  function processNext() {

  if (curPic==Pictures.length -1)
  {
    curPic=0;
  }
  else
  {
    curPic++;
  }
    document.myPicture.src=Pictures[curPic];
  }
  </SCRIPT>
</HEAD>

  <body MS_POSITIONING="GridLayout">
    <form name="Form1" method="post"
      action="RegisterStartupScript.aspx" id="Form1">
    <input type="hidden" name="__VIEWSTATE"
    value="dDwtMTE5MjkxMzIxODs7Pnsz8J7gSudeOCbOOvZN97mHZmky" />

    <img id="myPicture" name="myPicture" src="/ASPNETVB/1mages/ac1.jpg" />

    <input type="submit" name="BackButton" value="Back" id="BackButton"
      onClick="processPrevious();return false;" />

    <input type="submit" name="NextButton" value="Next" id="NextButton"
      onClick="processNext();return false;" />
```

```
    <script language="javascript">
    <!--
      var Pictures =  new
Array('Images/ac1.jpg','Images/ac2.jpg','Images/ac3.jpg');
    // -->
  </script>

  <!-- Here is the script generated by RegisterStartupScript method. -- >
  <script language='JavaScript'>alert('Hi');processNext()</script>
  </form>
  </body>
</HTML>
```

Using the RegisterOnSubmitStatement Method

You can use this method to process the JavaScript code when the form is submitted. This method is smarter than the RegisterStartupScript method because it actually wires your JavaScript code with the onSubmit event of the Form tag. Sometimes we wish the RegisterStartupScript method was also smart enough to wire the input JavaScript code with the onLoad event of the Body tag, but then, sometimes we wonder if we're obsessing too much with JavaScript. You be the judge!

Anyway, Listing 3-9 shows the code to demonstrate the RegisterOnSubmitStatement method. Notice how we put the call to this method outside the If Not Page.IsPostBack block. If we place it inside the block, JavaScript will only run once when the page is first loaded and it will not run during any post-back event.

Listing 3-9. The Server-Side Code to Inject JavaScript Code for the OnSubmit Event

```
Private Sub Page_Load(ByVal sender As System.Object, _
  ByVal e As System.EventArgs) Handles MyBase.Load

    Page.RegisterOnSubmitStatement("OnSubmit", "alert('Hi')")
End Sub
```

When the page is submitted, it displays a message box that says "Hi." Listing 3-10 shows the resulting HTML.

Listing 3-10. The JavaScript Generated by the RegisterOnSubmitStatement Method

```
<HTML>
    <HEAD>
        <title>Register OnSubmit Statement</title>
    </HEAD>

    <body>
        <form name="Form1" method="post" action="RegisterOnSubmit.aspx"
            language="javascript" onsubmit="alert('Hi')" id="Form1">

        <input type="hidden" name="__VIEWSTATE"
            value="dDwtMTE5MjkxMzIxODs7Plvmv42JXAKEeCggBfgdCV/a0djj" />
        </form>
    </body>
</HTML>
```

Removing JavaScript Code Programmatically

If you use any of the previously mentioned methods to generate JavaScript code programmatically, you can also remove them simply by calling the method(s) again and passing an empty string.

For example, if you want to remove the JavaScript alert that was included when we called the RegisterOnSubmitStatement, simply call it again and pass an empty string, as shown following. You will notice that the resulting HTML will not have the onSubmit event wiring inside the Form tag.

```
Page.RegisterOnSubmitStatement("OnSubmit", "")
```

Summary

This chapter focused on teaching various ways to generate JavaScript code dynamically. It also warned you that using these methods can be dangerous and risky, especially later, when you debug or enhance existing code. We would like to reiterate the best practice of organizing all client-side JavaScript code in the form of reusable functions and storing them in one or many .js files. You should leverage dynamic JavaScript generation reluctantly and only where absolutely needed.

CHAPTER 4

Handling Data Effectively

THIS CHAPTER COVERS VARIOUS ways in which to handle data effectively in a .NET application. We will start our discussion with the DataSet object, focusing on its features and limitations. We will then proceed to examining several other ways in which to handle data by using custom-built objects and collections. The goal of this chapter is to educate you, the reader, on the best ways to manage data with and without using a built-in and generic data structure, such as DataSet.

Handling Data by Using DataSet

The first few times we looked at the DataSet object, we felt as though looks could kill—DataSet could be the "killer application" for the next generation of Web sites. It seemed to have everything: complete support for in-memory data caching, change history, an elaborate data retrieval and persistence mechanism, and a disconnected nature. The more we used it on real-life applications, however, the more we began to learn about its limitations. After completing several .NET projects, we found ourselves not using it as much as we had before. Even though we don't use it as often anymore, we still find it to be a useful tool if it's employed appropriately. In this chapter, we share our experiences in the hopes that you will learn about the reality of working with DataSet before you actually use it on real-life applications.

An Inherent Problem with DataSet

An inherent problem with DataSet is that it provides a mechanism for structuring data without providing support for the business logic that needs to use that data. The .NET framework is object-oriented, as are the applications built with this framework. In an object-oriented world, objects represent business entities that encapsulate not only data but also business logic. Separating the data from the logic is inherently not an object-oriented approach.

Without a native support for business logic, we have found it advantageous to enhance the DataSet object to provide such support. It may seem like extra effort at the beginning of the project, but it has always paid off during the later stages.

To explain how separating data from business logic can affect your application, we will create two versions of a small application. One version will use the DataSet object in its pure form, and the other version will wrap it with business objects. During the course of this exercise, we will point out the pros and cons to these approaches.

Using the Raw DataSet to Create a Vendor Management System

Let's create a simple vendor management application to manage a list of companies and contact information. The purpose of this exercise is to demonstrate the abilities of the DataSet object and point out its strengths and weaknesses.

Figure 4-1 shows the example vendor management system.

Company Name :			
Contact Name :			
Contact Title :			Add

CustomerID	CompanyName	ContactName	ContactTitle
ALFKI	Alfreds Futterkiste	Maria Anders	Sales Representative
ANATR	Ana Trujillo Emparedados y helados	Ana Trujillo	Owner
ANTON	Antonio Moreno Taquería	Antonio Moreno	Owner
AROUT	Around the Horn	Thomas Hardy	Sales Representative
BERGS	Berglunds snabbköp	Christina Berglund	Order Administrator
BLAUS	Blauer See Delikatessen	Hanna Moos	Sales Representative

Figure 4-1. Snapshot view of the vendor management system

As you can see in Figure 4-1, the contact management system contains a data grid control that displays customer ID, company name, contact name, and title. We are also able to add a new contact by providing the company and contact information and clicking the Add button. Before we add a new contact, however, we need to apply the business rules listed in Table 4-1.

Table 4-1. Business Rules for the Vendor Management System

Rule 1	Company Name and Contact Name fields cannot be empty.
Rule 2	N/A or NA is not an acceptable value for the Company Name and Contact Name fields.
Rule 3	Check whether a customer's contact name already exists in the database before inserting a new customer.

As we said earlier, the DataSet object doesn't help encapsulate business rules, forcing us to provide a separate mechanism to maintain such rules. You will see in the following example that we provide methods in the user interface class to apply such rules. It can be argued that we could have created a new class to encapsulate such rules so that they can be reused on other windows, but even if we extract such rules out of the user interface and place them in a separate class, the fact remains that the business rules stay separate from the data to which they are applied.

In Listing 4-1, we create a method to check the validity of input fields. If such fields are not acceptable according to business rules 1 and 2, we will show an error message by using a label control. If input fields are acceptable, we will check whether a matching record already exists in the database according to business rule 3. If the contact already exists, we will show an error message by using a label control. Once all three rules are validated, we will proceed with adding the record to the database.

Listing 4-1. Applying Business Rules on a Raw DataSet Object

```
' The following method is called when Add button is pushed.
Private Sub AddButton_Click(ByVal sender As System.Object, _
                        ByVal e As System.EventArgs) Handles AddButton.Click

    Dim CustomersDS As DataSet
    Dim NewRow As DataRow

    ' The GetCustomers() method will look for customer's DataSet in
    ' cache first. If not found in cache, it will retrieve it from
    ' the database.
    CustomersDS = GetCustomers()
    NewRow = CustomersDS.Tables(0).NewRow()

    ' Populating the record with input fields.
    NewRow("CompanyName") = CompanyNameTextBox.Text
    NewRow("ContactName") = ContactNameTextBox.Text
    NewRow("ContactTitle") = ContactTitleTextBox.Text

    ' Checking to see if input data is acceptable by calling the
    ' CheckValidity() method. This methods applies business rules 1 and 2,
    ' mentioned previously.
    If CheckValidity(NewRow) = False Then
        Return
    End If
```

```vb
            ' If the customer doesn't already exist, adding it to the DataSet.
            ' The IsCustomerExist() method searches the DataSet for matching
            ' record. It returns true if matching record is found; otherwise, it
            ' returns false.
            If IsCustomerExist(CustomersDS, NewRow) = False Then
                CustomersDS.Tables(0).Rows.Add(NewRow)
                CustomersDataGrid.DataSource = CustomersDS.Tables(0).DefaultView
                CustomersDataGrid.DataBind()
            Else
                ErrorLabel.Text = "This customer already exists."
            End If
    End Sub


    Private Function GetCustomers() As DataSet
        Dim CustomerInfo As DataSet

        If Cache("CustomersDS") Is Nothing Then
            ' Getting customer's DataSet from database by using the
            ' predefined data access layer (DAL) class. The DAL
            ' class simply contains ADO.NET code to access database.
            CustomerInfo = DAL.GetCustomersDS()

            ' Inserting the newly retrieved DataSet in cache.
            Cache.Insert("CustomersDS", CustomerInfo)
        Else
            ' Retrieving the DataSet from cache.
            CustomerInfo = CType(Cache("CustomersDS"), DataSet)
        End If


        Return CustomerInfo
    End Function


    Private Function CheckValidity(ByVal aRow As DataRow) As Boolean
        ' Checking to see if customer name is provided.
        If IsEmpty(aRow, "CompanyName") = True Then
            ErrorLabel.Text = "Company Name is not acceptable."
            Return False
        End If

        ' Checking to see if contact name is provided.
        If IsEmpty(aRow, "ContactName") = True Then
            ErrorLabel.Text = "Contact Name is not acceptable."
            Return False
        End If
```

```
            Return True
    End Function


    Private Function IsEmpty(ByVal aRow As DataRow, _
                          ByVal fieldName As String) As Boolean

        If aRow(fieldName) Is Nothing Then
              Return True
        End If

        If aRow(fieldName) Is System.DBNull.Value Then
              Return True
        End If

        Dim FieldValue As String
        FieldValue = Convert.ToString(aRow(fieldName))

        If FieldValue = "" Then
              Return True
        End If

        ' NA or N/A is not an acceptable value.
        If FieldValue.ToUpper() = "NA" Or _
           FieldValue.ToUpper() = "N/A" Then
              Return True
        End If

        Return False
    End Function

    Private Function IsCustomerExist(ByVal CustomersDS As DataSet, _
               ByVal NewRow As DataRow) As Boolean
        Dim Row As DataRow

        For Each Row In CustomersDS.Tables(0).Rows
            If Row("CompanyName").ToString() = NewRow("CompanyName").ToString() And _
               Row("ContactName").ToString() = NewRow("ContactName").ToString()Then

                  Return True
            End If
        Next

        Return False
    End Function
```

CAUTION *What's wrong with the code shown in Listing 4-1? There is nothing functionally wrong with it; it functions as desired. It checks the validity of input fields and then checks to see if a customer already exists in the database.*

However, this code has several design issues. The biggest problem is that the code that applies business rules on the data is disconnected from the data, requiring us to pass the data as input parameters. This sort of design can lead to failure if the input data is passed in a structure that is different than the one the methods expect to receive.

Conceptually, this code is also not very object-oriented, because it doesn't allow us to think of customers in the form of self-sufficient objects. Instead, it forces us to treat customers as nothing more than raw data.

Handling Data by Using Business Objects: A Better Approach

You have heard a lot about why we need to encapsulate data and surround it with business rules so that we can treat the information as business objects instead of raw data. Let's see how you can achieve this purpose and still use all the built-in DataSet functionality.

In Listing 4-2, we show you the Customers class. This class allows the rest of the application to treat customer information as a business object by encapsulating customer-related data, as well as business rules.

Listing 4-2. Encapsulating a DataSet Object in the Customers Class

```
Imports System.Data
Imports System.Data.SqlClient

Public Class Customers
    Private _Data As DataTable

    Public ReadOnly Property Data() As IList
        Get
            Return _Data.DefaultView
        End Get
    End Property
```

```
Sub New()
    _Data = New DataTable("Customers")
End Sub


Public Sub Fill(ByVal adapter As SqlDataAdapter)
    adapter.Fill(_Data)
End Sub


Public Sub Update(ByVal adapter As SqlDataAdapter)
    adapter.Update(_Data)
End Sub


Public Sub Remove(ByVal customer As DataRow)
    _Data.Rows.Remove(customer)
End Sub


Public Sub RemoveAt(ByVal index As Integer)
    _Data.Rows.RemoveAt(index)
End Sub


Public Function NewCustomer() As DataRow
    Return _Data.NewRow()
End Function


Public Function GetCustomer(ByVal index As Integer) As DataRow
    Return _Data.Rows(index)
End Function
```

```
End Class
```

You can see in Listing 4-2 that the Customers class uses a private member variable of type DataTable. Because all customer information can be contained in one table, there is no need to encapsulate a DataSet object. Encapsulating a DataSet object in this example will create unnecessary complexity in the code and not provide much value. If you need a business object that contains information from more than one table, you can consider using the DataSet object instead. Otherwise, we recommend that you stick with a DataTable.

An interesting thing about the Customers class is that it exposes the data contained in the DataTable by using the IList interface, which is key to maintaining the encapsulation. The users of the Customers class don't really need to know the format this class uses to store its information. All they need to know is how to access the information. The IList interface provides a lot of flexibility, including the capability to bind the information to web controls using built-in data binding features, as well as the capability to use the for-each loop to iterate through the information. This interface is further discussed later in this chapter in the section "The Magic Is Still with the IList Interface."

BEST PRACTICE *Use the IList interface generously!*
The IList interface is used a lot in the .NET framework. As a matter of fact, when you bind a DataView object to a Web control, the Web control uses the IList interface to bind the data. As a result, we can bind any object to any Web control as long as the object supplies the IList interface.

The IList interface inherits from the IEnumerable interface, which allows you to use a for-each loop. The IList interface also combines the ICollection interface, which gives it the features that we have come to expect from any .NET array such as Add, Remove, RemoveAt, IndexOf, Insert, Contains, and Clear.

A True Story About IList!

At this point, I would like to take a minute to share with you a true story related to the IList interface. Not too long ago, during one of my projects, I had created a custom business object that encapsulated product information. I chose to expose the product list by using an IList interface similar to the way the Customers class exposes its customer information. I was under the impression that the programmer responsible for creating the Web pages could simply data bind to my custom business object by using the IList interface it supplied. Little did I know that I was assuming too much about the programmer's knowledge of the data binding mechanism. To make a long story short, I learned a little too late that the Web page programmer consistently used a for-each loop to iterate through the product information I supplied, only to create a temporary DataTable object, which he used to bind to the data grid.

Moral of the story: Know your interfaces and how the ASP.NET Web controls use them.

—Farhan Muhammad

Now that we know how the Customers object exposes its information, let's take a look at the methods it provides.

Methods of the Customers Class

The Customers class provides the following methods: Constructor, Fill, Update, Remove, RemoveAt, NewCustomer, and GetCustomer.

The Constructor method simply instantiates the DataTable object so that it can start with an empty list.

The Fill method receives a data adapter object and uses it to retrieve information from the database to populate the DataTable. It is not this class's responsibility to know how to retrieve the information. In a typical n-tier application, such responsibility resides with the data access tier. The business objects simply need a mechanism by which they can retrieve data from its source. This design allows the business objects to be oblivious of the mechanism used to access the physical data source, providing the capability to change the physical data source in the future (if needed) without affecting business objects.

 NOTE   *The .NET framework also uses this approach to prevent the DataSet object from having any knowledge of the physical data source.*

Similarly, the Update method also uses the data adapter object to persist its changes to the physical database.

The Remove and RemoveAt methods simply forward the call to the Remove and RemoveAt methods of the DataTable object, respectively. Remember, the Customers class is simply a wrapper on the DataTable object.

The NewCustomer method creates a new DataRow object by using the internal DataTable object and returns the newly created DataRow object to the caller. The Customers object can use this method to create an empty customer record, fill it with the information, and call the AddCustomer method, shown in the next section, to add a new customer to the list.

The GetCustomer method receives an array index and returns the customer record found at a specified index. Just like its counterparts, this method also reuses the internal DataTable object to find the matching DataRow object at the specified index.

Now that we have seen how easy it is to wrap the basic DataTable functionality inside a custom-created object, it's time to turn our attention to adding business rules to the Customers class.

Adding Business Rules to the Customers Class

It is time now to start adding business logic to the Customers class. After all, the main reason we created the Customers class is to provide a way to encapsulate such business logic. The fact that we also chose to encapsulate the DataTable object to reuse its functionality is an added bonus.

Listing 4-3 shows the business logic contained in the Customers class. You will recognize the CheckValidity, IsEmpty, and IsCustomerExists methods from Listing 4-1, where we had to keep these methods in the code-behind file. We discussed in Chapter 1 why code behind is not meant for storing business or data logic code. We also discussed that the purpose of code-behind file is only to contain the user interface implementation logic needed to make sure that the user interface responds to user interaction in a desired fashion.

Listing 4-3. Business Logic Contained in the Customers Class

```
Public Class Customers
    Private _Data As DataTable

#Region "DataTable encapsulation"
    Public ReadOnly Property Data() As IList
        Get
            Return _Data.DefaultView
        End Get
    End Property

    Sub New()
        _Data = New DataTable("Customers")

    End Sub

    Public Sub Fill(ByVal adapter As SqlDataAdapter)
        adapter.Fill(_Data)
    End Sub

    Public Sub Update(ByVal adapter As SqlDataAdapter)
        adapter.Update(_Data)
    End Sub

    Public Sub Remove(ByVal customer As DataRow)
        _Data.Rows.Remove(customer)
    End Sub
```

```
    Public Sub RemoveAt(ByVal index As Integer)
        _Data.Rows.RemoveAt(index)
    End Sub

    Public Function NewCustomer() As DataRow
        Return _Data.NewRow()
    End Function

    Public Function GetCustomer(ByVal index As Integer) As DataRow
        Return _Data.Rows(index)
    End Function

#End Region

#Region "Business Logic"
    ' This method adds a new customer to the list.
    Public Sub AddCustomer(ByVal CompanyName As String, _
                           ByVal ContactName As String, _
                           ByVal ContactTitle As String)

        Dim NewCustomer As DataRow

        ' Getting an empty new data row.
        NewCustomer = Me.NewCustomer()

        ' Filling customer information data row by using input parameters.
        NewCustomer("CompanyName") = CompanyName
        NewCustomer("ContactName") = ContactName
        NewCustomer("ContactTitle") = ContactTitle

        ' Redirecting to overloaded AddCustomer method.
        Me.AddCustomer(NewCustomer)

    End Sub

    Public Sub AddCustomer(ByVal newCustomer As DataRow)

        ' Checking to see if input data is valid by calling a private method.
        CheckValidity(newCustomer)

        ' Checking to see if customer already exists by calling a
        ' private method named IsCustomerExist.
```

```vb
        If IsCustomerExist(newCustomer) = False Then
            ' If customer does not exist, adding it to the list.
            _Data.Rows.Add(newCustomer)
        Else
    ' If customer exists, throwing CustomerExistException. This
            ' exception is defined following.
            Throw New CustomerExistException()
        End If

End Sub


Public Sub UpdateCustomer(ByVal index As Integer, _
                                        ByVal customer As DataRow)
    ' Checking to see if input data is valid by calling a private method.
    CheckValidity(customer)

    ' Everything is good; updating customer information.
    _Data.Rows(index).ItemArray = customer.ItemArray
End Sub


Private Sub CheckValidity(ByVal customer As DataRow)
    ' Checking to see if customer name is provided by calling a
    ' private method named IsEmpty, which applies business rules 1 and 2.
    If IsEmpty(customer, "CompanyName") = True Then
    ' Business rule 1 or 2 failed; throwing an exception.
        Throw New CustomerNameRequiredException()
    End If

    ' Checking to see if contact name is provided by calling a
    ' private method named IsEmpty, which applies business rules 1 and 2.
    If IsEmpty(customer, "ContactName") = True Then
        ' Business rule 1 or 2 failed; throwing an exception.
        Throw New ContactNameRequiredException()
    End If
End Sub


Private Function IsEmpty(ByVal customer As DataRow, _
        ByVal fieldName As String) As Boolean

    ' Applying business rules 1 and 2 by checking to see if desired
    ' value in input data row is either empty or contains N/A.
    If customer(fieldName) Is Nothing Then
    ' Field is uninitialized.
        Return True
```

```vbnet
        ElseIf customer(fieldName) Is System.DBNull.Value Then
            ' Field contains null.
                Return True
        ElseIf Convert.ToString(customer(fieldName)) = "" Then
            ' Field contains empty string.
                Return True
        ElseIf Convert.ToString(customer(fieldName)).ToUpper() = "N/A" Then
            ' Field contains N/A.
                Return True
        ElseIf Convert.ToString(customer(fieldName)).ToUpper() = "NA" Then
            ' Field contains NA.
                Return True
        Else
        ' Field contains a valid value.
                Return False
        End If
    End Function


    Private Function IsCustomerExist(ByVal newCustomer As DataRow) As Boolean
        Dim Row As DataRow

        ' Checking to see if customer already exists in the list,
        ' according to business rule 3.
    For Each Row In _Data.Rows
    If Row("CompanyName").ToString() = newCustomer("CompanyName").ToString() And _
        Row("ContactName").ToString() = newCustomer("ContactName").ToString() Then

' Found a customer record with matching customer name
' and contact name.
                Return True
            End If
        Next

        Return False
    End Function


#End Region
End Class


' Defining exceptions that are thrown by the Customers class.
' Any Customers class user can catch these exceptions to
' handle errors as business rules are applied by this class.
```

```
Public Class CustomerExistException
    Inherits System.Exception
    Public Sub New()
        MyBase.New("Customer already exists!")
    End Sub

End Class

Public Class CustomerNameRequiredException
    Inherits System.Exception
    Public Sub New()
        MyBase.New("Customer name is required!")
    End Sub
End Class

Public Class ContactNameRequiredException
    Inherits System.Exception
    Public Sub New()
        MyBase.New("Contact name is required!")
    End Sub
End Class
```

The approach of encapsulating business logic in a custom-created class might look like extra work to you. It not only requires us to write the wrapper code for the internal DataTable object, but it also forces us to think about business rules and to design ways to apply these rules from the very start. In all our experience using the .NET framework to handle situations like the one shown in the preceding examples, the approach of encapsulating business logic and the raw DataSet together in a custom-created object has always proven to be a success.

This approach results not only in the capability to reuse the maximum amount of code, it also paves the way for creating code that can be maintained easily. By using this approach, we can add new business rules or modify or remove existing business rules easily at one spot, without affecting the rest of the application.

This approach also results in easily extensible code. Because the Customers class users only care about making method calls to its member functions, we can easily reuse this class throughout the application (or potentially in other applications). To understand how easy it is to use the Customers class in the Web pages, consider the example in Listing 4-4.

Listing 4-4. Using the Customers Class in a Web Page

```vb
' The AddButton_Click method is called when user tries to enter a

' new customer record.
Private Sub AddButton_Click(ByVal sender As System.Object, _
                ByVal e As System.EventArgs) Handles AddButton.Click

        Dim CustomerInfo As Customers

        ' Calling GetCustomers method to get an instance of Customers class.
        CustomerInfo = GetCustomers()

                ' Calling the AddCustomer method of Customers class to add a new
                ' customer record. We are also handling exceptions if they are
                ' thrown as the Customers class applies its business rules.
                Try
                        CustomerInfo.AddCustomer(CompanyNameTextBox.Text, _
                                ContactNameTextBox.Text, _
                                ContactTitleTextBox.Text)

                        ' Rebinding customers data grid to show newly added record.
                        CustomersDataGrid.DataSource = CustomerInfo.Data
                        CustomersDataGrid.DataBind()

                Catch expAlreadyExist As CustomerExistException
                        ' Showing error message from the exception object.
                        ErrorLabel.Text = expAlreadyExist.Message
                Catch expNameRequired As CustomerNameRequiredException
                        ' Showing error message from the exception object.
                        ErrorLabel.Text = expNameRequired.Message
                Catch expContactRequired As ContactNameRequiredException
                        ' Showing error message from the exception object.
                        ErrorLabel.Text = expContactRequired.Message
                End Try

End Sub

Private Function GetCustomers() As Customers
        Dim CustomerInfo As Customers
```

```vb
        ' Checking for Customers object in cache.
        If Cache("Customers") Is Nothing Then
                ' Not found in cache; creating a new object from the database.
                CustomerInfo = DAL.GetCustomers()
                Cache.Insert("Customers", CustomerInfo)
        Else
                CustomerInfo = CType(Cache("Customers"), Customers)
        End If

    Return CustomerInfo
End Function


' The DAL (Data Access Layer) class is responsible for executing
' SQL statements or stored procedures on physical database.
Public Class DAL

    ' The GetCustomers method retrieves customer information from
    ' the database, fills Customers object, and returns this newly
    ' created Customers object.
    Public Shared Function GetCustomers() As Customers
        Dim CustomerInfo As New Customers()

        Dim MyConnection As New SqlConnection()
        Dim MyCommand As New SqlCommand()
        Dim MyAdapter As New SqlDataAdapter()

        MyConnection.ConnectionString = AppSettings.Get("DSN")
        MyCommand.CommandText = "Select CustomerID, CompanyName," + _
                        " ContactName, ContactTitle " + _
                        " from Customers"
        MyCommand.Connection = MyConnection

        MyAdapter.SelectCommand = MyCommand

        ' Filling Customers object with the result set by calling its
        ' Fill method and passing a data adapter object to it.
        CustomerInfo.Fill(MyAdapter)

        Return CustomerInfo
    End Function

End Class
```

We hope that you can see the value of creating custom business objects for the purpose of maintaining a group of information. As we said earlier in the chapter, the approach of using just the raw DataSet to manipulate data directly is not necessarily the wrong approach. If all you need to do is collect and display data and don't have much need for applying business rules to the database, then the raw DataSet approach can be the right choice for you.

As we stated earlier, our intent throughout this chapter is to show you alternative approaches to handling data and associated business rules effectively. Choosing the approach that fits your needs resides solely with you and your team.

Handling Data by Using Strongly Typed Collections

Just when you thought you learned everything there is to know about handling data effectively, we are throwing you another curve ball. Before you decide to start building your application by using the last approach we showed you, where we encapsulated a DataTable object inside a custom business object, take a look at this next approach.

We don't always have to use the DataTable or DataSet objects while handling data. We have seen it time and again that programmers new to the .NET framework tend to use (and abuse) these two objects extensively. There are other alternatives, and these alternatives work just as effectively as the built-in DataSet or DataTable objects. In fact, these alternatives can be an even better solution in some cases. Specifically, when you need to pass data over a Remoting boundary, whether by a Web service or binary serialization, custom objects are serialized in smaller sizes and transfer more efficiently than the built-in and quite bulky DataSet and DataTable objects.

Getting to Know the CollectionBase Class

The .NET framework provides a very useful class: CollectionBase. This class, found under the System.Collections namespace, is your best friend! We recommend that you get to know this class very well. It will open your eyes and make you believe that there is more to data handling than DataSet.

As its name suggests, the CollectionBase class is meant to be the parent class for your customized collection. You can create your own class that can inherit from this class to acquire basic collection style functionality. Take a look at any or all of your data needs and we can tell you from our experience that you can solve most of them with a good collection object. Let's take our customer management system as an example. All we need is a way to manage a collection of customer records. If you can have the ability to add, remove, insert, update, and search for specific customer records, you will effectively have everything you need from the DataTable object without actually having to use this object. The

CollectionBase class provides most of this functionality out-of-the-box, and we can easily customize it to add features.

Another benefit we get by using the CollectionBase class is that we can strongly type our records. A very few programmers I know like to use the Table.Rows[index].Cells[index].Value style of programming. By using the CollectionBase class, you can write your code as Collection[index].Property. The former approach doesn't provide the type of the value you are accessing. Because of this limitation, you will always be required to check for and convert the type before you use the value. The latter approach clearly specifies the type of value you are trying to access, simply because properties in your custom class return a specific type of value. In the following discussion, we will show you examples of how a strongly typed object is far better than a loosely typed data row.

Let's rewrite our small application without using a DataTable object. Listing 4-5 shows how to use the CollectionBase class to create a list of custom business objects.

Listing 4-5. Using a CollectionBase Class to Create a List of Custom Business Objects

```
' We are creating a collection object that will contain a list of objects
' instantiated from Customer class. This collection class inherits from
' the CollectionBase class to provide basic list management features.
 Public Class CustomerCollection
     Inherits CollectionBase
     Public Sub New()
         MyBase.New()
     End Sub
End Class


' The Customer class represents a single customer record.
Public Class Customer

    ' Private member variables.
    Private _CompanyName As String
    Private _ContactName As String
    Private _ContactTitle As String

    ' Public properties.
    Public Property CompanyName() As String
        Get
            Return _CompanyName
        End Get
        Set(ByVal Value As String)
            _CompanyName = Value
        End Set
    End Property
```

```
Public Property ContactName() As String
    Get
        Return _ContactName
    End Get
    Set(ByVal Value As String)
        _ContactName = Value
    End Set
End Property


Public Property ContactTitle() As String
    Get
        Return _ContactTitle
    End Get
    Set(ByVal Value As String)
        _ContactTitle = Value
    End Set
End Property


' Constructor for creating empty customer record.
Public Sub New()
    _CompanyName = ""
    _ContactName = ""
    _ContactTitle = ""
End Sub


' Constructor for creating customer record from a data reader object.
Public Sub New(ByVal Reader As IDataReader)
    Me.New(Reader("CompanyName"), _
            Reader("ContactName"), _
            Reader("ContactTitle"))

End Sub


' Constructor for creating customer record by passing parameter values.
Public Sub New(ByVal CompanyName As String, _
            ByVal ContactName As String, _
            ByVal ContactTitle As String)
    _CompanyName = CompanyName
    _ContactName = ContactName
    _ContactTitle = ContactTitle
End Sub


End Class
```

The code example shown in Listing 4-5 would work for basic list management functionality. Now that we've gone through the hassle of creating a custom business object, however, we now need to make the collection strongly typed. A *strongly typed collection* contains data in its own field and exposes it to properties that return objects of specific types instead of generic "object" types. A strongly typed collection helps the compiler to check types to make sure our code accesses the data by using appropriate data types and, hence, reduce the risks of failure when the code executes.

BEST PRACTICE *When we say that we need to use a strongly typed collection object, we mean that we need to provide methods that receive objects of specific types for collection management purposes. For example, a strongly typed collection receives a specific type of object as an input parameter to its Add method instead of the generic "Object" type parameter.*

You may recall from Listing 4-1, where we used the DataRowCollection object, that it receives and returns generic "Object" types. The problem with the generic types is that you as a programmer will always have to do extra work to determine the real type of the object and perform the appropriate type conversion as necessary. Failure to perform the correct type conversion often results in weak and error-prone code.

A strongly typed collection makes code more robust by receiving and returning objects of a specific type. For instance, our CustomerCollection class should receive and return objects of type Customer to be a strongly typed collection.

In the next section, we'll show you how to make the CustomerCollection class in this example strongly typed.

Making CustomerCollection Strongly Typed

The CustomerCollection class shown in Listing 4-5 is not yet a strongly typed collection. To make this collection strongly typed, we need to implement methods provided by the IList interface. This interface is supported by the CollectionBase class, which also provides a generic implementation of this interface.

Listing 4-6 shows the strongly typed implementation of the IList interface. This example should help you understand the concept of strongly typed programming.

Listing 4-6. Making CustomerCollection a Strongly Typed Collection

```
Public Class CustomerCollection
    Inherits CollectionBase
    Public Sub New()
        MyBase.New()
    End Sub


#Region "Creating strongly typed collection by implementing IList interface"

    ' Implementing Insert method to receive object of Customer class
    ' instead of generic object of type "Object."
    ' InnerList is the private member used by the CollectionBase class
    ' to maintain the list. It is an object of type "ArrayList."
    Public Sub Insert(ByVal index As Integer, ByVal NewCustomer As Customer)
        InnerList.Insert(index, NewCustomer)
    End Sub


    ' Implementing Remove method to receive object of Customer class
    ' instead of generic object of type "Object."
    Public Sub Remove(ByVal aCustomer As Customer)
        InnerList.Remove(aCustomer)
    End Sub


    ' Implementing Contains method to receive object of Customer class
    ' instead of generic object of type "Object."
    Public Function Contains(ByVal aCustomer As Customer) As Integer
        Return InnerList.Contains(aCustomer)
    End Function


    ' Implementing IndexOf method to receive object of Customer class
    ' instead of generic object of type "Object."
    Public Function IndexOf(ByVal aCustomer As Customer) As Integer
        Return InnerList.IndexOf(aCustomer)
    End Function


    ' Implementing Add method to receive object of Customer class
    ' instead of generic object of type "Object."
    Public Function Add(ByVal NewCustomer As Customer) As Integer
        Return InnerList.Add(NewCustomer)
    End Function

#End Region

End Class
```

Now that you have looked at the last two code examples carefully, you know that we have created a strongly typed Customer class to create a single customer record and a strongly typed CustomerCollection class to maintain the list of Customer objects.

Let's keep enhancing the CustomerCollection class by adding business rules. Remember, we developed three business rules earlier in this chapter as presented in Table 4-1. Business rules 1 and 2 require that we don't accept empty customer records while adding a new record to the list. Rule 3 requires us to check whether the customer record already exists before inserting it.

Listing 4-7 shows you how we can add these business rules in the CustomerCollection class. I would recommend that you start comparing the code in the IsEmpty and ValidityCheck methods shown in this example with their counterparts shown in Listing 4-3. You will soon start to see how strongly typed objects help you develop robust and easy-to-maintain program code.

Listing 4-7. Adding Business Rules in the CustomerCollection Class

```
Public Class CustomerCollection
    Inherits CollectionBase
    Public Sub New()
        MyBase.New()
    End Sub


    ' We added the following constructor to provide us with the ability to
    ' populate this collection by using a data reader object.
    ' The reason we used IDataReader interface is to reduce our reliance on
    ' a specific managed provider.
    Public Sub New(ByVal Reader As IDataReader)
        Me.Fill(Reader)
    End Sub


    Public Sub Fill(ByVal Reader As IDataReader)
        While (Reader.Read() = True)
            Dim aCustomer As New Customer(Reader)
            Me.Add(aCustomer)
        End While
    End Sub


#Region "Creating strongly typed collection"

    Public Sub Insert(ByVal index As Integer, ByVal NewCustomer As Customer)
        ' Check to see if input data is valid (business rules 1 and 2).
        CheckValidity(NewCustomer)
```

```
            ' If the customer doesn't already exist, add it (business rule 3).
            If IsCustomerExist(NewCustomer) = False Then
                InnerList.Insert(index, NewCustomer)
            Else
                Throw New CustomerExistException()
            End If
    End Sub


    Public Sub Remove(ByVal aCustomer As Customer)
        InnerList.Remove(aCustomer)
    End Sub


    Public Function Contains(ByVal aCustomer As Customer) As Integer
        Return InnerList.Contains(aCustomer)
    End Function


    Public Function IndexOf(ByVal aCustomer As Customer) As Integer
        Return InnerList.IndexOf(aCustomer)
    End Function


    Public Function Add(ByVal NewCustomer As Customer) As Integer
        ' Check to see if input data is valid (business rules 1 and 2).
        CheckValidity(NewCustomer)

        ' If the customer doesn't already exist, add it (business rule 3).
        If IsCustomerExist(NewCustomer) = False Then
            Return InnerList.Add(NewCustomer)
        Else
            Throw New CustomerExistException()
        End If
    End Function


#End Region


#Region "Business Rules"


    ' This method applies business rule 3, which requires us to check
    ' whether the customer record already exists before adding a new record.

    ' Because this collection is now strongly typed, it receives the new
    ' customer record as an object of Customer type instead of as a generic
    ' DataRow.
    Private Function IsCustomerExist(ByVal newCustomer As Customer) _
As Boolean
        Dim aCustomer As Customer
```

```
        ' This for-each loop iterates through all customer records contained
        ' in this collection.
        For Each aCustomer In Me
                ' Notice how we used the CompanyName and ContactName properties
                ' to compare company name and contact name.
                ' In Listing 4-3, where we received
                ' customer record as DataRow object, we had to perform complex
                ' type conversion before comparing these values.
                If aCustomer.CompanyName = newCustomer.CompanyName And _
                    aCustomer.ContactName = newCustomer.ContactName Then

                    Return True
                End If
        Next

        Return False
    End Function


    Private Sub CheckValidity(ByVal aCustomer As Customer)
        ' Checking to see if customer name is provided.
        If IsEmpty(aCustomer.CompanyName) = True Then
            Throw New CustomerNameRequiredException()
        End If

        ' Checking to see if contact name is provided.
        If IsEmpty(aCustomer.ContactName) = True Then
            Throw New ContactNameRequiredException()
        End If
    End Sub


    Private Function IsEmpty(ByVal Field As String) As Boolean

        ' Compare this method with its counterpart in the loosely
        ' typed collection class shown in Listing 4-3. You will find
        ' that strongly typed objects are much easier to use and provide
        ' a more robust solution.

        If Field Is Nothing Then
            Return True
        ElseIf Field Is System.DBNull.Value Then
            Return True
        ElseIf Field = "" Then
            Return True
        ElseIf Field.ToUpper() = "N/A" Then
            Return True
```

```
        ElseIf Field.ToUpper() = "NA" Then
            Return True
        Else
            Return False
        End If
    End Function
```

```
#End Region
```

```
End Class
```

You can easily bind the strongly typed CustomerCollection class shown in Listing 4-7 to any ASP.NET Web server controls. You can also use it to iterate through the list by using the for-each loop. The strongly typed implementation of the IList interface allows you to add a new customer object, remove an existing customer object, and search for a customer object with ease.

Using a Strongly Typed Collection with ASP.NET Server Controls

We are sure that some of you are wondering about the usefulness of the strongly typed collection that we just created. It is normal to expect it to provide at least as many features as its counterpart Customers class, which was built with an encapsulated DataTable object. Actually, the strongly typed CustomerCollection class provides most of the functionality of a DataTable, except for its sorting and filtering capabilities. It also doesn't keep a history of changes made to the collection. If you really want these features and still want to use the strongly typed collection, you will have to create these features on your own. C'mon now, don't be scared! It is not as difficult to add these features as you might think. In fact, we will demonstrate the ease of adding such functionality by modifying the CustomerCollection class in next few examples. Hang on, and keep reading!

Listing 4-8 shows you how we used this strongly typed collection to bind to the data grid Web server control.

Listing 4-8. Using a Strongly Typed Collection to Bind to a Web Server Control

```
' When the page loads, we call the GetCustomers method to receive
' an object of CustomerCollection class. We simply bind this object
' to the data grid Web control.
Private Sub Page_Load(ByVal sender As System.Object, _
        ByVal e As System.EventArgs) Handles MyBase.Load
    Dim MyCustomers As CustomerCollection
```

```
                ' Calling GetCustomers to receive CustomerCollection object.
          MyCustomers = GetCustomers()

                ' Because CustomerCollection class inherits from CollectionBase class,
                ' we simply bind it to the Web server control.
          CustomersDataGrid.DataSource = MyCustomers
          CustomersDataGrid.DataBind()
       End Sub

       ' The AddButton_Click method executes when user clicks the Add
       ' button to add a new customer to the list.
       Private Sub AddButton_Click(ByVal sender As System.Object, _
    ByVal e As System.EventArgs) Handles AddButton.Click

          Dim MyCustomers As CustomerCollection

                ' Calling GetCustomers to receive an object of CustomerCollection.
          MyCustomers = GetCustomers()

          Try
                ' Creating a new Customer object and populating its fields by
                ' using its properties. Compare this approach with the difficulty
                ' associated with populating DataRow object, and we guarantee that
                ' you will never want to use DataTable again.
             Dim NewCustomer As New Customer()
             NewCustomer.CompanyName = CompanyNameTextBox.Text
             NewCustomer.ContactName = ContactNameTextBox.Text
             NewCustomer.ContactTitle = ContactTitleTextBox.Text
                ' Adding the newly created Customer object to the
                ' CustomerCollection object simply by calling its Add method.
             MyCustomers.Add(NewCustomer)

             CustomersDataGrid.DataSource = MyCustomers
             CustomersDataGrid.DataBind()

          Catch expAlreadyExist As CustomerExistException
                ' Show additional information from the exception object.
             ErrorLabel.Text = expAlreadyExist.Message
          Catch expNameRequired As CustomerNameRequiredException
                ' Show additional information from the exception object.
             ErrorLabel.Text = expNameRequired.Message
          Catch expContactRequired As ContactNameRequiredException
                ' Show additional information from the exception object.
             ErrorLabel.Text = expContactRequired.Message
```

```
        End Try
    End Sub


    ' The GetCustomer method first checks to see if CustomerCollection object
    ' exists in cache. If not, it calls a data access method to obtain it
    ' from the database.
    Private Function GetCustomers() As CustomerCollection
        Dim MyCustomers As CustomerCollection

        If Cache("Customers") Is Nothing Then
            ' Customer collection is not in cache, getting it from database.
            MyCustomers = DAL.GetCustomersCollection()
            Cache.Insert("Customers", MyCustomers)
        Else
            MyCustomers = CType(Cache("Customers"), CustomerCollection)
        End If

        Return MyCustomers
    End Function


' The data access layer (DAL) class provides a method to retrieve customer
' information from the database by using the data reader object and populate
' the CustomerCollection object with it.
Public Class DAL
    Public Shared Function GetCustomersCollection() As CustomerCollection

        Dim MyConnection As New SqlConnection()
        Dim MyCommand As New SqlCommand()
        Dim MyCustomers As New CustomerCollection()
        Dim MyReader

        MyConnection.ConnectionString = AppSettings.Get("DSN")
        MyCommand.CommandText = "Select CustomerID, CompanyName," + _
                                " ContactName, ContactTitle " + _
                                " from Customers"
        MyCommand.Connection = MyConnection
        MyCommand.Connection.Open()
        MyReader = MyCommand.ExecuteReader()

        ' Passing the data reader to the Fill method of CustomerCollection
        ' class, which will use this data reader to populate its internal
        ' list of Customer objects.
        MyCustomers.Fill(MyReader)
```

```
        ' Returning fully populated CustomerCollection object.
        Return MyCustomers
    End Function
End Class
```

The code in Listing 4-8 attempts to show how easy it is to use a strongly typed collection. We wouldn't be surprised if you told us that you didn't know that a custom object could be bound directly to a Web server control. In our experience, we have seen that most beginning-to-intermediate ASP.NET programmers believe that the only way to populate the server controls is to use a DataTable or a data view object. As a matter of fact, we have been in situations where Web programmers used the strongly typed collection only to loop through its content and create a temporary DataTable object, which they later used to bind to the server control.

We can still use the IList interface to make the custom collection bindable to an ASP.NET server control, as we'll see next.

The Magic Is Still with the IList Interface

We discussed earlier in this chapter that the Web server controls access bindable objects only via their IList interface. In Listing 4-2, where we encapsulated a DataTable object inside a custom-created Customers object, we chose to return the data contained in the DataTable object by using the IList interface.

The custom-created strongly typed collection, if inherited from the CollectionBase class, also implements the IList interface. In fact, any object that inherits from the CollectionBase class automatically implements the IList interface. Whether we choose to customize the IList interface implementation depends on our desire to strongly type a collection object. In the case of the CustomerCollection class shown in Listing 4-8, we chose to strongly type the IList implementation by providing custom methods that received and returned objects of the Customer class.

Because any object inherited from the CollectionBase class automatically implements the IList interface, you can bind it to the Web server controls just the way you would bind a data view object.

Adding a Search Mechanism to the Strongly Typed Collection

Some would argue that a great benefit of using the DataTable object is its ability to filter records, and we would agree. We have often encountered similar situations where we were interested in only some of the records contained in the collection and not all.

By default, the strongly typed collection won't provide a filter mechanism. However, you can easily create such a feature just by adding a few extra lines of code, as shown in Listing 4-9.

Listing 4-9. Adding a Filtering Capability to the Strongly Typed CustomerCollection Class

```
Public Class CustomerCollection
    Inherits CollectionBase
    Public Sub New()
        MyBase.New()
    End Sub

    Public Sub New(ByVal Reader As IDataReader)
        Me.Fill(Reader)
    End Sub

    Public Sub Fill(ByVal Reader As IDataReader)
        While (Reader.Read() = True)
            Dim aCustomer As New Customer(Reader)
            Me.Add(aCustomer)
        End While
    End Sub

' The code related to IList implementation and business rules are removed
' for clarity.

#Region "Providing filtering capabilities"

    Public Function FilterByCompany(ByVal aCompanyName As String) _
                    As CustomerCollection

        Dim aCustomer As Customer
        Dim NewCollection As CustomerCollection

  ' Looping through the collection to find customers with matching
  ' company name. Once found, adding the customer object to
  ' a new collection.
  For Each aCustomer In Me
            If aCustomer.CompanyName = aCompanyName Then
                NewCollection.Add(aCustomer)
            End If
        Next
```

```
            Return NewCollection

    End Function

    Public Function FilterByContact(ByVal aContactName As String) _
                                            As CustomerCollection

        Dim aCustomer As Customer
        Dim NewCollection As CustomerCollection

  ' Looping through the collection to find customers with matching
  ' contact name. Once found, adding the customer object to
  ' a new collection.
        For Each aCustomer In Me
            If aCustomer.ContactName = aContactName Then
                NewCollection.Add(aCustomer)
            End If
        Next

        Return NewCollection

    End Function
#End Region

End Class
```

As you can see in Listing 4-9, filtering the collection can be as simple as looping through the internal list and collecting the objects that have matching information. This mechanism works fine for smaller lists. If you are working with a larger collection, for example, a collection of more than 1,000 objects, you might want to consider optimizing the search mechanism by using a number of search algorithms. However, a sequential search is often satisfactory for small collections.

Adding Row State Capability to the Strongly Typed Collection

One great benefit of the DataTable object is its ability to maintain row state flags for its records. This capability allows us to filter the record to obtain only the changed records, or just the deleted records, etc.

In Listing 4-10, we show you how you can enhance the previously created strongly typed collection to have such functionality. This example starts by showing a modified version of the Customer class. Because this class effectively serves as the counterpart to the data row class, this is the appropriate place for us to add the row state flag. Once we make the Customer class aware of its change state, we will enhance the CustomerCollection class to provide the ability to filter the records to obtain just those that were changed after being retrieved from the database.

Listing 4-10. Adding Row State Capability to the Customer Collection

```
Public Class Customer

    Private _CompanyName As String
    Private _ContactName As String
    Private _ContactTitle As String

    ' Adding a flag to contain row state.
    Private _RowState As Char

    ' Providing read-only property for retreiving row state.
    Public ReadOnly Property RowState()
        Get
            Return _RowState
        End Get
    End Property

    ' All public properties mark the object with updated "U" flag
    ' in their Set clauses.
    Public Property CompanyName() As String
        Get
            Return _CompanyName
        End Get
        Set(ByVal Value As String)
            _CompanyName = Value

            ' Marking the object as updated.
            _RowState = "U"
        End Set
    End Property

    Public Property ContactName() As String
        Get
            Return _ContactName
        End Get
        Set(ByVal Value As String)
            _ContactName = Value
```

```
                ' Marking the object as updated.
                _RowState = "U"
        End Set
End Property


Public Property ContactTitle() As String
    Get
            Return _ContactTitle
    End Get
    Set(ByVal Value As String)
        _ContactTitle = Value

            ' Marking the object as updated.
            _RowState = "U"
    End Set
End Property


Public Sub New()
    _CompanyName = ""
    _ContactName = ""
    _ContactTitle = ""

    ' Marking the object as newly created.
    _RowState = "N"
End Sub


Public Sub New(ByVal Reader As IDataReader)
    Me.New(Reader("CompanyName"), _
            Reader("ContactName"), _
            Reader("ContactTitle"))

End Sub


Public Sub New(ByVal CompanyName As String, _
            ByVal ContactName As String, _
            ByVal ContactTitle As String)
    _CompanyName = CompanyName
    _ContactName = ContactName
    _ContactTitle = ContactTitle

    ' Marking the object as newly created.
    _RowState = "N"

End Sub
```

```vb
    ' Adding the Delete method to provide the ability to mark this
    ' object as deleted.
    Public Sub Delete()
        _RowState = "D"
    End Sub

End Class

Public Class CustomerCollection
    Inherits CollectionBase
    Public Sub New()
        MyBase.New()
    End Sub

    Public Sub New(ByVal Reader As IDataReader)
        Me.Fill(Reader)
    End Sub

    Public Sub Fill(ByVal Reader As IDataReader)
        While (Reader.Read() = True)
            Dim aCustomer As New Customer(Reader)
            Me.Add(aCustomer)
        End While
    End Sub

    ' The GetChangedRecords method loops through all objects in the list
    ' and returns a new collection containing only the changed objects.
    Public Function GetChangedRecords() As CustomerCollection

        Dim aCustomer As Customer
        Dim NewCollection As CustomerCollection

        For Each aCustomer In Me
            ' Filtering the list by changed objects.
            If aCustomer.RowState = "U" Then
                NewCollection.Add(aCustomer)
            End If
        Next

        Return NewCollection

    End Function
End Class
```

Providing the Ability to Sort the Strongly Typed Collection

As most of you know, it is very useful to have the capability to sort a collection based on any given property. For example, having the capability to sort customer records by company name, contact name, or contact title would allow us to leverage the column-sorting events that the data grid control provides. It is quickly becoming a standard for any grid-type display to provide a mechanism for sorting the list by clicking a column heading.

You should be glad to know that the CollectionBase class already provides a mechanism for us to sort the list. However, because this class is designed to be a generic class, it doesn't know how to compare custom-created properties. Our responsibility, to leverage the built-in sort mechanism, is to provide a mechanism to compare values. Once we develop a mechanism to compare property values, we can let the built-in sort mechanism do the rest.

To provide a mechanism to compare property values, we are required to create a class that implements the IComparer interface. The IComparer interface is defined in the System.Collections namespace. It consists of just one method, Compare. The Compare method receives two objects as input parameters and returns an integer value. The integer value should be 0 if both objects are equal, greater than 0 if the first object is greater, and less than 0 if the first object is less.

In Listing 4-11, we create three comparer classes to compare the properties of the Customer class.

Listing 4-11. Creating the Three Comparer Classes

```
' This class provides mechanism for comparing CompanyName property.
Public Class CompanyNameComparer
    Implements IComparer

    Function Compare(ByVal x As Object, ByVal y As Object) As Integer _
                    Implements IComparer.Compare

        Dim CustomerX As Customer
        Dim CustomerY As Customer

        ' Converting generic input objects to the objects of Customer class.
        CustomerX = CType(x, Customer)
        CustomerY = CType(y, Customer)

        ' Comparing CompanyName property and returning comparison result.
        Return CustomerX.CompanyName = CustomerY.CompanyName

    End Function
End Class
```

```vbnet
' This class provides mechanism for comparing ContactName property.
Public Class ContactNameComparer
    Implements IComparer

    Function Compare(ByVal x As Object, ByVal y As Object) As Integer _
                    Implements IComparer.Compare

        Dim CustomerX As Customer
        Dim CustomerY As Customer

        ' Converting generic input objects to the objects of Customer class.
        CustomerX = CType(x, Customer)
        CustomerY = CType(y, Customer)

        ' Comparing ContactName property and returning comparison result.
        Return CustomerX.ContactName = CustomerY.ContactName

    End Function
End Class

' This class provides mechanism for comparing ContactTitle property.
Public Class ContactTitleComparer
    Implements IComparer

    Function Compare(ByVal x As Object, ByVal y As Object) As Integer _
                    Implements IComparer.Compare

        Dim CustomerX As Customer
        Dim CustomerY As Customer

        ' Converting generic input objects to the objects of Customer class.
        CustomerX = CType(x, Customer)
        CustomerY = CType(y, Customer)

        ' Comparing ContactTitle property and returning comparison result.
        Return CustomerX.ContactTitle = CustomerY.ContactTitle

    End Function
End Class
```

```vbnet
' Enhancing CustomerCollection class to provide sorting capabilities.
Public Class CustomerCollection
    Inherits CollectionBase
    Public Sub New()
        MyBase.New()
    End Sub

    Public Sub New(ByVal Reader As IDataReader)
        Me.Fill(Reader)
    End Sub

    Public Sub Fill(ByVal Reader As IDataReader)
        While (Reader.Read() = True)
            Dim aCustomer As New Customer(Reader)
            Me.Add(aCustomer)
        End While
    End Sub

#Region "Sorting the collection"
    Public Sub Sort(ByVal propertyName As String)

        If propertyName.ToUpper() = "COMPANYNAME" Then
            ' Using company name comparer to sort by CompanyName.
            Dim Comparer As New CompanyNameComparer()
            InnerList.Sort(Comparer)
        ElseIf propertyName.ToUpper() = "CONTACTNAME" Then
            ' Using contact name comparer to sort by ContactName.
            Dim Comparer As New ContactNameComparer()
            InnerList.Sort(Comparer)
        ElseIf propertyName.ToUpper() = "CONTACTTITLE" Then
            ' Using contact title comparer to sort by ContactTitle.
            Dim Comparer As New ContactTitleComparer()
            InnerList.Sort(Comparer)
        End If
    End Sub
#End Region

End Class
```

Summary

We have said everything we wanted to say about maintaining data by using the .NET framework. We are sure that some of you may be overwhelmed by the amount of information presented in this chapter. Some of you may be a little confused about which method to use for your next project.

After years of experience programming with a variety of technologies, including the .NET framework, we have come to realize that there is no one right way to program to manage data in a .NET application. We are not going to point at any one of the previously mentioned methods and tell you to use it in all cases. We have learned enough to realize that every situation is unique and every situation deserves a solution that best suits its needs.

We will, however, provide you with a few guidelines for choosing the right method for your needs. If all you need is to retrieve data from the database and bind it to a control, we suggest that you use the built-in DataSet or DataTable objects. If you don't need to work directly with the data much or don't have any business rules to apply, why bother with creating custom objects and incurring extra code development and maintenance overhead? You should always weigh benefits against cost. If you feel that the cost of creating custom business objects outweighs the benefits you need to receive, don't use this method. In this case, we recommend that you stick with handling raw data by using the built-in DataSet or DataTable objects and focus on spending your time and energy on other areas of your application.

If you need to apply business rules, we recommend that you consider creating custom business object(s) by either encapsulating a DataTable object or inheriting from the CollectionBase class. Here, you will need to weigh cost versus benefits once again. If you need to handle a large amount of information and need to provide search and sort functionality, you will be better off encapsulating a DataTable or DataSet object. As you saw in previous examples, the CollectionBase class doesn't provide built-in searching and comparing mechanisms, which requires that you custom write this code. The search feature alone can consume a significant amount of your time if you desire an elaborate searching mechanism. If you are working with a large number of records, then you might desire faster searches. In this case, we recommend that you accept the complexity associated with using loosely typed and generic data row objects to obtain the benefits of handling a large number of records effectively.

Moral of the story: Understand your options, and use your weapons wisely.

CHAPTER 5

Using ASP.NET to Manage Lists

WE WOULD BE RICH if we had a dime for every time we saw ASP.NET list management controls used inappropriately, particularly the repeater, data list, and data grid controls. These awesome ASP.NET features can also be ASP.NET's biggest problems, causing programmers to spend countless nights chasing the productivity mirage. The stories are the same everywhere, especially when they relate to the data grid control. So many programmers relentlessly pursue the rewards from this fruitful control only to find themselves cornered with a control that offers limited customization and performs poorly.

The problem with these controls, especially the data grid control, is that they seem to be a good idea at the beginning but often prove to be problematic if used inappropriately. This problem grows by multiple orders of magnitude when many ASP.NET books fail to caution the readers on the proper use of such controls. In this chapter, we focus on showing the pitfalls of these controls and teaching how to avoid these pitfalls. We urge you to read on if you want to learn to program like the experts and achieve the productivity and performance gains that these controls promise.

Before we start, let us tell you that when it comes to these controls, one size doesn't fit all. Stop forcing the data grid control to solve all your list management problems. It is not the best thing since sliced bread. It is slow, is not very flexible, and bloats the view state size. Having said that, we would also like to compliment the data grid control for the tasks it performs nicely, such as paging, sorting, and inline data editing.

Let's start by comparing performance differences between the data grid, data list, and repeater controls. Once you have seen the impact of these controls on performance, you might be more inclined to use the control that provides the maximum amount of performance gains without compromising desired functionality for your particular situation.

Data Binding Performance Differences

The examples that follow show the most commonly used techniques for reading a list of records from a relational database and binding the result set to a list management control. We will show you three variations, each using a different type of list management control. We will first start with the data grid object mainly because most programmers tend to use this object as their first weapon of choice. It is easy to use, visually configurable, and feature-rich. However, most programmers don't know that this control performs extremely poorly compared to its counterparts. The two subsequent examples will show the performance differences that occur when you perform the same task by using a data list control and a repeater.

Data Binding Performance of the Data Grid Control

Let's start this comparison of data binding performance by looking at the data grid control. Listing 5-1 shows an HTML segment that contains a data grid control.

Listing 5-1. HTML That Contains a Data Grid Control

```
<%@ Page language="c#" Codebehind="DataGridWithInlineDataBinding.aspx.cs"
AutoEventWireup="false" Inherits="ASPControls.DataGridWithInlineDataBinding" %>
<!DOCTYPE HTML PUBLIC "-//W3C//DTD HTML 4.0 Transitional//EN" >
<HTML>
  <body MS_POSITIONING="GridLayout">
    <form id="DataGridWithInlineDataBinding" method="post" runat="server">
<asp:DataGrid id=CustomerDataGrid runat="server">
<HeaderStyle Font-Bold="True" HorizontalAlign="Center" VerticalAlign="Top"
BackColor="LightGray">
</HeaderStyle>
</asp:DataGrid>
      </form>
  </body>
</HTML>
```

The HTML code shown in Listing 5-1 simply creates a data grid server control on the page. It doesn't have any fancy template columns, sorting, paging, etc. Not everyone needs to use these advanced features. In fact, in our experience, we have seen more data grid implementations that do not use the advanced features. In such cases, programmers often pay a performance penalty without redeeming it by reaping other benefits. Listing 5-2 shows the code behind for the HTML we saw in Listing 5-1.

Listing 5-2. Retrieving a List of Records from the Database and Binding It to the CustomerDataGrid Control

```
public class DataGridWithInlineDataBinding : System.Web.UI.Page
   {
       protected System.Web.UI.WebControls.DataGrid CustomerDataGrid;
       private void Page_Load(object sender, System.EventArgs e)
       {
     // Data binding when page is loaded.
           CustomerDataGrid.DataSource = GetLargeDS().Tables[0].DefaultView;
           CustomerDataGrid.DataBind();
       }


   // The function selects 100 records from the Northwind database and returns
   // a data view object containing the result set.
       public DataSet GetLargeDS()
       {
           DataSet MyDataSet = new DataSet();
           SqlDataAdapter MyAdapter = new SqlDataAdapter();

           SqlCommand MyCommand = new SqlCommand();
           MyCommand.Connection = new
     SqlConnection(System.Configuration.ConfigurationSettings.AppSettings["dsn"]);
           MyAdapter.SelectCommand = MyCommand;

           MyCommand.Connection.Open();
           MyCommand.CommandText = " select top 100 Orders.OrderID," +
               " Customers.CompanyName, Employees.LastName," +
               " Employees.FirstName, Orders.OrderDate," +
               "Orders.RequiredDate, Orders.ShippedDate" +
               " from Orders, Customers, Employees" +
               " where Orders.CustomerID = Customers.CustomerID" +
               " and Orders.EmployeeID = Employees.EmployeeID";

           MyAdapter.Fill(MyDataSet, "OrderList");

           MyCommand.Connection.Close();
           MyCommand.Connection.Dispose();
           MyCommand.Dispose();

           return MyDataSet;
       }
}
```

There is nothing special about the code shown in Listing 5-2. It is your typical everyday data access code. It has been done hundreds of time in dozens of different ways. Our goal here is not to evaluate data access codes but to understand the data binding overhead that is associated with the data grid control. If you are interested in learning best practices for the data management code, we suggest that you read Chapter 4, which focuses exclusively on handling data by using a variety of mechanisms.

Let's take a look at the performance result when we execute the code shown in Listing 5-2 by using the Application Center Test (ACT). The tests were written to run the maximum number of users for 60 seconds on a Pentium III 1.2 GHz system with 512 MB of RAM. We are sure that most production servers use faster hardware, but our goal is to compare performance results among various code variations on a consistent hardware platform. The performance result for the data grid control example is shown in Figure 5-1.

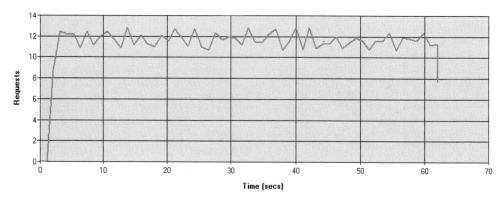

Figure 5-1. Performance test result for using a data grid control and simple data binding via the code behind

The graph itself doesn't show much except for the fact that the server ran an average of 12 simultaneous requests every second. However, this graph will prove to be much more important when we show you other code variations and their impact on performance.

Data Binding Performance of the Data List Control

The data list control is simpler than the data grid control, requiring you to provide your own template for header, footer, item, alternate item, etc. Listing 5-3 uses the data list control instead of the data grid control to display a list of records.

Listing 5-3. Using a Data List Control to Display a List of Records from a Database

```
<HTML>
<body MS_POSITIONING="GridLayout">
<form id=DataListWithInlineDataBinding method=post runat="server">
<asp:datalist id=CustomerDataList runat="server">
<HeaderTemplate>
    <tr bgcolor=lightgrey valign=top>
    <th> </th>
    <th>Order ID</th>
    <th>Company Name</th>
    <th>Last Name</th>
    <th>First Name</th>
    <th>Order Date</th>
    <th>Required Date</th>
    <th>Shipped Date</th>
    </tr>
</HeaderTemplate>
<ItemTemplate>
<TR valign="top" align="left"><TD>
<TD><%#DataBinder.Eval(Container.DataItem, "OrderID")%></TD>
<TD><%#DataBinder.Eval(Container.DataItem, "CompanyName")%></TD>
<TD><%#DataBinder.Eval(Container.DataItem, "LastName")%></TD>
<TD><%#DataBinder.Eval(Container.DataItem, "FirstName")%></TD>
<TD><%#DataBinder.Eval(Container.DataItem, "OrderDate")%></TD>
<TD><%#DataBinder.Eval(Container.DataItem, "RequiredDate")%></TD>
<TD><%#DataBinder.Eval(Container.DataItem, "ShippedDate")%></TD></TR>
</ItemTemplate>
</asp:datalist></form> </body>
</HTML>
```

The HTML code shown in Listing 5-3 is a little more complex than the code we used for the data grid control. It provides programmers with more flexibility to control the information layout and, in turn, requires a few lines of extra work. Does it make the data list a better control? Some of you might argue that controls that are easier to use contribute to greater gains in productivity, and you would be correct.

However, a good software designer looks at more than one feature. Everything is subjective in defining a good software design practice, which leads to just one conclusion. A good software design is one that serves your needs now and your needs in the foreseeable future. The key word here is "foreseeable." Programmers too often get tied up in trying to create the best engineered solution regardless of how academic it might be. Our rule has been to program for today, account for tomorrow, and stop looking ahead. The fact is that users' requirements for a software system change very fast. It is almost impossible to predict what you might be asked to program four months from now, let alone a year or two later. Considering such facts, programming your system now to provide next year's benefits does not seem like a productive use of your time, unless next year's benefits are clearly seen and understood by all parties involved.

 BEST PRACTICE *A good software design is one that serves your current needs and the needs of the foreseeable future. For example, if you need the fastest performing applications and are willing to compromise on productivity, then a solution that emphasizes productivity gains while incurring performance loss is not a good solution. However, such a design could be a perfect solution for smaller applications made by less-experienced individuals for whom productivity rates higher than performance.*

Listing 5-4 shows C# code to retrieve 100 records from the Northwind database and display it on the page by using the data list control shown in Listing 5-3.

Listing 5-4. Displaying Database Records Onscreen by Using a Data List Control

```csharp
public class DataListWithInlineDataBinding : System.Web.UI.Page
{
    protected System.Web.UI.WebControls.DataList CustomerDataList;

    private void Page_Load(object sender, System.EventArgs e)
    {
        CustomerDataList.DataSource = GetLargeDS().Tables[0].DefaultView;
        CustomerDataList.DataBind();
    }

    // The function selects 100 records from the Northwind database and returns
    // a data view object containing the result set.
    public DataSet GetLargeDS()
    {
        DataSet MyDataSet = new DataSet();
        SqlDataAdapter MyAdapter = new SqlDataAdapter();

        SqlCommand MyCommand = new SqlCommand();
        MyCommand.Connection = new
SqlConnection(System.Configuration.ConfigurationSettings.AppSettings["dsn"]);
        MyAdapter.SelectCommand = MyCommand;
```

```
MyCommand.Connection.Open();

MyCommand.CommandText = " select top 100 Orders.OrderID," +
    " Customers.CompanyName, Employees.LastName," +
    " Employees.FirstName, Orders.OrderDate," +
    "Orders.RequiredDate, Orders.ShippedDate" +
    " from Orders, Customers, Employees" +
    " where Orders.CustomerID = Customers.CustomerID" +
    " and Orders.EmployeeID = Employees.EmployeeID";

MyAdapter.Fill(MyDataSet, "OrderList");

MyCommand.Connection.Close();
MyCommand.Connection.Dispose();
MyCommand.Dispose();

return MyDataSet;
    }
}
```

Once again, there is nothing very special about this code. It simply retrieves a list of 100 records from the Northwind database and displays it on the page by binding the result set to the data list control. Let's look at Figure 5-2 to see if the data list control performs more efficiently than the data grid control. This graph is also generated by using the ACT, just as the graph for Figure 5-1 was generated.

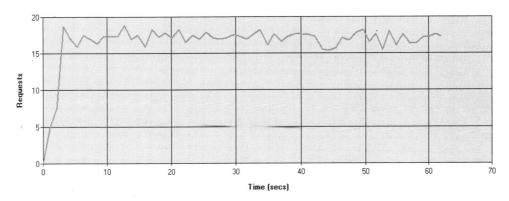

Figure 5-2. Performance test result for using simple data binding via the code behind to bind data to a data list control

There you have it! The data list control performed about 30 percent faster than the data grid control. It is able to serve about 17 requests per second as compared to 12 with the data grid. So, what does it mean in real life? It means lower hardware costs and happier customers. Basically, using a data list control can enable you to accommodate more customers on a particular hardware system and infrastructure than you could by using a data grid control. The collapse of dot-com companies in the late nineties and the following recession have executives thinking long and hard about cost savings, especially when related to hardware and infrastructure.

These examples are a little misleading, we must admit. In most real-life scenarios, the HTML for a data grid control won't be this simple. In fact, most professional data grid users use template columns, which make the code just as complex as it is with the data list control. Unless you need to use a feature that is specific to the data grid control, we suggest that you use the data list control instead. The data list control has another nice feature that allows you to control repeat columns, repeat direction, and repeat format. We have used this feature several times to provide very pleasant and graphically enhanced Web sites.

Data Binding Performance of the Repeater Control

The repeater control gives you the most amount of flexibility while you develop your Web page. On the other hand, it is also the most complex of the three controls we are discussing, requiring you to custom build just about everything but a loop. Let's look at Listing 5-5 to see a variation that uses the repeater control instead of the data list or data grid control.

Listing 5-5. Using a Repeater Control to Display a List of Records from a Database

```
<HTML>
    <body MS_POSITIONING="GridLayout">
    <form id="Repeater" method="post" runat="server">
        <asp:Repeater id=CustomerRepeater runat="server">
            <HeaderTemplate>
                <table>
                        <tr bgcolor=lightgrey valign=top>
                        <th>Order ID</th>
                        <th>Company Name</th>
                        <th>Last Name</th>
                        <th>First Name</th>
                        <th>Order Date</th>
                        <th>Required Date</th>
                        <th>Shipped Date</th>
                        </tr>
                </HeaderTemplate>
```

```
        <ItemTemplate>
            <tr valign=top align=left>
                <td><%#DataBinder.Eval(Container.DataItem, "OrderID")%></td>
                <td><%#DataBinder.Eval(Container.DataItem, "CompanyName")%></td>
                <td><%#DataBinder.Eval(Container.DataItem, "LastName")%></td>
                <td><%#DataBinder.Eval(Container.DataItem, "FirstName")%></td>
                <td><%#DataBinder.Eval(Container.DataItem, "OrderDate")%></td>
                <td><%#DataBinder.Eval(Container.DataItem, "RequiredDate")%></td>
                <td><%#DataBinder.Eval(Container.DataItem, "ShippedDate")%></td>
            </tr>
        </ItemTemplate>
        <FooterTemplate>
            </table>
        </FooterTemplate>
      </asp:Repeater>
   </form>
  </body>
</HTML>
```

The repeater code looks similar to the data list code. However, the difference between the data list and repeater is that the data list provides many more features. The extent of the repeater's features has almost been reached in this example. Let's look at Listing 5-6 to see the C# code for retrieving 100 records from the Northwind database and displaying them onscreen by using the repeater control.

Listing 5-6. Displaying Database Records Onscreen by Using a Repeater Control

```
public class RepeaterWithInlineDataBinding : System.Web.UI.Page
{
    protected System.Web.UI.WebControls.Repeater CustomerRepeater;

    private void Page_Load(object sender, System.EventArgs e)
    {
        CustomerRepeater.DataSource = GetLargeDS().Tables[0].DefaultView;
        CustomerRepeater.DataBind();
    }

    // The function selects 100 records from the Northwind
    // database and returns a data view object containing
    // the result set.
    public DataSet GetLargeDS()
```

```
    {
        DataSet MyDataSet = new DataSet();
        SqlDataAdapter MyAdapter = new SqlDataAdapter();

        SqlCommand MyCommand = new SqlCommand();
        MyCommand.Connection = new
SqlConnection(System.Configuration.ConfigurationSettings.AppSettings["dsn"]);

        MyAdapter.SelectCommand = MyCommand;
        MyCommand.Connection.Open();

        MyCommand.CommandText = " select top 100 Orders.OrderID," +
            " Customers.CompanyName, Employees.LastName," +
            " Employees.FirstName, Orders.OrderDate," +
            " Orders.RequiredDate, Orders.ShippedDate" +
            " from Orders, Customers, Employees" +
            " where Orders.CustomerID = Customers.CustomerID" +
            " and Orders.EmployeeID = Employees.EmployeeID";

        MyAdapter.Fill(MyDataSet, "OrderList");

        MyCommand.Connection.Close();
        MyCommand.Connection.Dispose();
        MyCommand.Dispose();

        return MyDataSet;
    }
}
```

Once again, the code is quite simple and ordinary. Most importantly, it is consistent with the code for the previous two examples. This consistency helps to ensure that the performance results are not affected by anything else except by the server controls themselves. The performance result is shown in Figure 5-3. This graph is generated by using the ACT.

The repeater solution seems to run even faster than the data list solution. It is able to support about 22 requests per second as compared to 17 for the data list control and 12 for the data grid control. However, we also learned that the repeater is the lightest of all controls. It really doesn't provide much built-in functionality except for a built-in loop. A repeater solution will require extra coding work, creating extra complexity. We suggest that you use this type of solution only when a data list control turns out to be too slow for your needs.

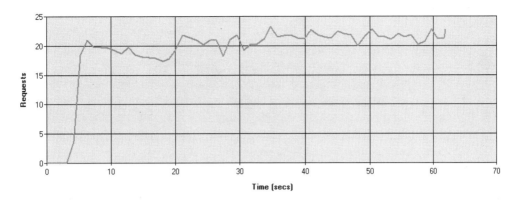

Figure 5-3. Performance result for using a repeater control to bind 100 records from the database

Let's look at Figure 5-4 to compare performance differences between the data grid, data list, and repeater controls.

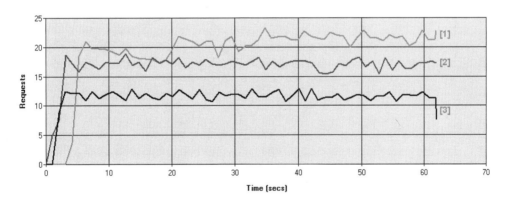

Figure 5-4. Comparison of performance results from all three solutions. Option 1 is the repeater solution, option 2 is the data list solution, and option 3 is the data grid solution.

BEST PRACTICE   *Of the three solutions shown in Figure 5-4, we recommend that you consider the data list control as your first choice. Look at the data grid control only when you discover that data list doesn't provide a desired built-in feature. Similarly, you should use the repeater only when the data list control is too slow for your needs.*

Data Binding Techniques and Their Effects

We have so far used simple data binding techniques, where we let the controls use their default behavior. In most real-life examples, you would need to write some amount of custom code to make sure that the resulting Web page shows information in the most desirable format.

There are three common ways in which to format information during the data binding process: inline format expressions, event handlers, and member methods. In this section, we will examine each of these ways and conduct performance tests to determine the mechanism that is most efficient. Keep in mind, however, that performance is not the only measure. We will also discuss ease-of-use and maintainability effects to determine best practices.

Using an Inline Format Expression for Data Binding

The inline format expression is a commonly used mechanism featured in most ASP.NET books, articles, and sample code. With this mechanism, you can write inline code by using the <% %> tags to format the output during the data binding process. The inline format expression is mostly created by using the DataBinder.Eval method, which uses reflection to process the content contained in the list that is being bound to the control. This method receives the current item and format expression as input parameters. The current item is passed by the DataItem property of the Container object. The expression defines how to format the content before it appears on the page.

This method, though frequently used in books and articles, has a reputation for poor performance because it uses Reflection API. We will conduct performance tests by using this method and its counterparts as we move forward to demonstrate which method performs fastest among the three. Listing 5-7 shows an HTML code example that contains a repeater control and inline format expression.

Listing 5-7. Example of Data Binding by Using an Inline Format Expression

```
<HTML>
  <HEAD>
  <body MS_POSITIONING="GridLayout">
  <form id="Repeater" method="post" runat="server">
    <asp:Repeater id=CustomerRepeater runat="server">
```

```
<HeaderTemplate>
    <table>
        <tr bgcolor=lightgrey valign=top>
        <th>Order ID</th>
        <th>Company Name</th>
        <th>Last Name</th>
        <th>First Name</th>
        <th>Order Date</th>
        <th>Required Date</th>
        <th>Shipped Date</th>
        </tr>
</HeaderTemplate>
<ItemTemplate>
        <tr valign=top align=left>
        <td><%#DataBinder.Eval(Container.DataItem, "OrderID")%></td>
        <td><%#DataBinder.Eval(Container.DataItem, "CompanyName")%></td>
        <td><%#DataBinder.Eval(Container.DataItem, "LastName")%></td>
        <td><%#DataBinder.Eval(Container.DataItem, "FirstName")%></td>
        <td><%#DataBinder.Eval(Container.DataItem, "OrderDate")%></td>
        <td><%#DataBinder.Eval(Container.DataItem, "RequiredDate", "{0:d}")%></td>
        <td><%#DataBinder.Eval(Container.DataItem, "ShippedDate", "{0:d}")%></td>
        </tr>
</ItemTemplate>
<FooterTemplate>
</table>
</FooterTemplate>
</asp:Repeater>
</table>
</form>
</body>
</HTML>
```

The HTML shown in Listing 5-7 uses a repeater control to display a list of order information from the Northwind database. It uses the DataBinder.Eval method to format inline information. In fact, it applies default formatting to the order ID, company name, last name, first name, and order date column. Required date and shipped date columns, however, are formatted to show a short date string instead of the default long date string.

The HTML shown in Listing 5-7 uses the same code behind as shown in Listing 5-6, where the code simply queries the Northwind database to retrieve a data set of 100 records. This data set is then used to data bind to the repeater control. Figure 5-5 shows the output when this code is run. You will clearly see that the order date column uses the default date format of long date string, whereas the required date and shipped date columns show the short date string format.

Order ID	Company Name	Last Name	First Name	Order Date	Required Date	Shipped Date
10248	Vins et alcools Chevalier	Buchanan	Steven	7/4/1996 12:00:00 AM	8/1/1996	7/16/1996
10249	Toms Spezialitäten	Suyama	Michael	7/5/1996 12:00:00 AM	8/16/1996	7/10/1996
10250	Hanari Carnes	Peacock	Margaret	7/8/1996 12:00:00 AM	8/5/1996	7/12/1996
10251	Victuailles en stock	Leverling	Janet	7/8/1996 12:00:00 AM	8/5/1996	7/15/1996
10252	Suprêmes délices	Peacock	Margaret	7/9/1996 12:00:00 AM	8/6/1996	7/11/1996
10253	Hanari Carnes	Leverling	Janet	7/10/1996 12:00:00 AM	7/24/1996	7/16/1996
10254	Chop-suey Chinese	Buchanan	Steven	7/11/1996 12:00:00 AM	8/8/1996	7/23/1996
10255	Richter Supermarkt	Dodsworth	Anne	7/12/1996 12:00:00 AM	8/9/1996	7/15/1996

Figure 5-5. Result of data binding by using inline formatting

Using an Event Handler for Data Binding

Another way to format output during the data binding process is to capture an ItemDataBound event. This event is provided by the data grid, data list, and repeater controls, and it is raised once for each item that is being bound to the control. You can capture this event in two ways. You can declaratively capture it in the HTML syntax for the control by using the OnItemDataBound syntax. For example, the syntax for a repeater controller would look as follows:

```
<asp:Repeater id=CustomerRepeater OnItemDataBound="EventHandlerMethodName"
runat="server">
```

Another way to capture this event is to use the InitializeComponent method in the code-behind file. This method is automatically created for you if you use Visual Studio .NET. This method, which runs once every time the page is loaded in the memory on the Web server, is responsible for initializing all components used in the page and for wiring event handlers with appropriate events. The syntax for a wiring handler with the ItemDataBound event follows:

```
CustomerRepeater.ItemDataBound += new
    System.Web.UI.WebControls.RepeaterItemEventHandler(
                        CustomerRepeater_ItemDataBound);
```

CAUTION *If you are using C# to program your Web page, make sure to use either the declarative HTML syntax or the code-behind syntax, but do not use both. Using both methods calls the event handler twice. Visual Basic .NET programmers don't need to worry about this issue because Visual Basic .NET doesn't use the InitializeComponent method for event wiring. Instead, Visual Basic .NET uses the Handles keyword at the end of the method to wire the event handler.*

If you use the event handler to format the output, then you would have to use a server control to contain the content. Listing 5-5 showed a way to display content by using the DataBinder.Eval method that didn't require us to use a server control to place information retrieved from the database. However, if you plan to use code to manipulate the data, you will need to use ASP.NET server controls to contain the content.

In Listing 5-8, we show an HTML segment that uses a few label controls in the repeater control to serve as a placeholder for data that is retrieved from the database. We will later use the Text property of these label controls from the ItemDataBound event handler to provide it with appropriate content.

Listing 5-8. Using a Repeater Control That Contains Label Controls to Show Order Records

```
<asp:Repeater id=CustomerRepeater runat="server">
<HeaderTemplate>
    <table>
        <tr bgcolor=lightgrey valign=top>
        <th>Order ID</th>
        <th>Company Name</th>
        <th>Last Name</th>
        <th>First Name</th>
        <th>Order Date</th>
        <th>Required Date</th>
        <th>Shipped Date</th>
        </tr>
</HeaderTemplate>
<ItemTemplate>
        <tr valign=top align=left>
        <td><asp:label id=OrderIDLabel runat=server></asp:label></td>
        <td><asp:label id="CompanyNameLabel" runat=server></asp:label></td>
        <td><asp:label id="LastNameLabel" runat=server></asp:label></td>
        <td><asp:label id="FirstNameLabel" runat=server></asp:label></td>
        <td><asp:label id="OrderDateLabel" runat=server></asp:label></td>
        <td><asp:label id="RequiredDateLabel" runat=server></asp:label></td>
        <td><asp:label id="ShippedDateLabel" runat=server></asp:label></td>
        </tr>
</ItemTemplate>
<FooterTemplate>
    </table>
</FooterTemplate>
</asp:Repeater>
```

The HTML code example in Listing 5-8 shows a repeater control that uses labels to display order records instead of the DataBinder.Eval syntax. These labels are populated programmatically by using the event handler for the ItemDataBound event. The next example, shown in Listing 5-9, captures the ItemDataBound event and uses the event handler to retrieve appropriate data from the row that is being bound to the repeater control then uses this data to populate the label control.

Listing 5-9. C# Code-Behind Syntax to Show Data Using the ItemDataBound Event Handler

```csharp
public class RepeaterWithProgrammaticDataBinding : System.Web.UI.Page
{
    protected System.Web.UI.WebControls.Repeater CustomerRepeater;

    private void Page_Load(object sender, System.EventArgs e)
    {
        CustomerRepeater.DataSource = GetLargeDS().Tables[0].DefaultView;
        CustomerRepeater.DataBind();
    }

    // This method gets 100 records from the Northwind database and populates a
    // data set object.
    public DataSet GetLargeDS()
    {
        DataSet MyDataSet = new DataSet();
        SqlDataAdapter MyAdapter = new SqlDataAdapter();

        SqlCommand MyCommand = new SqlCommand();
        MyCommand.Connection = new
SqlConnection(System.Configuration.ConfigurationSettings.AppSettings["dsn"]);
        MyAdapter.SelectCommand = MyCommand;

        MyCommand.Connection.Open();

        MyCommand.CommandText = " select top 100 Orders.OrderID," +
            " Customers.CompanyName, Employees.LastName," +
            " Employees.FirstName, Orders.OrderDate," +
            "Orders.RequiredDate, Orders.ShippedDate" +
            " from Orders, Customers, Employees" +
            " where Orders.CustomerID = Customers.CustomerID" +
            " and Orders.EmployeeID = Employees.EmployeeID";

        MyAdapter.Fill(MyDataSet, "OrderList");
```

```
        MyCommand.Connection.Close();
        MyCommand.Connection.Dispose();
        MyCommand.Dispose();

        return MyDataSet;
}


override protected void OnInit(EventArgs e)
{
        InitializeComponent();
        base.OnInit(e);
}


private void InitializeComponent()
{
        // Wiring the event handler with the ItemDataBound event.
        CustomerRepeater.ItemDataBound +=
            new System.Web.UI.WebControls.RepeaterItemEventHandler(
                CustomerRepeater_ItemDataBound);
        this.Load += new System.EventHandler(this.Page_Load);
}


// This event handler is called for every record that is bound
// to the repeater control.
private void CustomerRepeater_ItemDataBound(object sender,
                        System.Web.UI.WebControls.RepeaterItemEventArgs e)
{
    // Not interested in an event if it is not fired for either the
    // items or the alternating items.
    if (e.Item.ItemType != ListItemType.Item &&
            e.Item.ItemType != ListItemType.AlternatingItem)
                return;

    // DataItem property of repeater item object returns the record that
    // is currently being bound to the repeater control.
    DataRowView BindedItem = e.Item.DataItem as DataRowView;

    // We are now ready to start populating the label controls that are
    // used to show the order record. First we have to find the label
    // control that we want to populate before we can set its text property.
    Label OrderIDLabel = e.Item.FindControl("OrderIDLabel") as Label;
    if (OrderIDLabel != null)
        OrderIDLabel.Text = BindedItem["OrderID"].ToString();
```

```
Label CompanyNameLabel = e.Item.FindControl("CompanyNameLabel") as Label;
if (CompanyNameLabel != null)
    CompanyNameLabel.Text = BindedItem["CompanyName"].ToString();


Label LastNameLabel = e.Item.FindControl("LastNameLabel") as Label;
if (LastNameLabel != null)
    LastNameLabel.Text = BindedItem["LastName"].ToString();


Label FirstNameLabel = e.Item.FindControl("FirstNameLabel") as Label;
if (FirstNameLabel != null)
    FirstNameLabel.Text = BindedItem["FirstName"].ToString();


Label OrderDateLabel = e.Item.FindControl("OrderDateLabel") as Label;
if (OrderDateLabel != null)
{
    DateTime OrderDate =
        Convert.ToDateTime(BindedItem["OrderDate"].ToString());
    OrderDateLabel.Text = OrderDate.ToString("d");
}


Label RequiredDateLabel = e.Item.FindControl("RequiredDateLabel") as Label;
if (RequiredDateLabel != null)
{
    DateTime RequiredDate =
        Convert.ToDateTime(BindedItem["RequiredDate"].ToString());
    RequiredDateLabel.Text = RequiredDate.ToString("d");
}


Label ShippedDateLabel = e.Item.FindControl("ShippedDateLabel") as Label;
if (ShippedDateLabel != null)
{
    DateTime ShippedDate =
        Convert.ToDateTime(BindedItem["ShippedDate"].ToString());
    ShippedDateLabel.Text = ShippedDate.ToString("d");
}
    }
}
```

The code shown in Listing 5-9 looks overly complicated. Most of the complications arise from the fact that the ItemDataBound event handler doesn't have a better way to access controls contained in the repeater control. The same problem exists if we choose to use the data list or data grid controls instead. Also, having to use the FindControl method to access controls contained inside the repeater slows down performance. You will see when we show performance results between the three mechanisms that this mechanism performs most poorly. Some of the performance issues with this method arise from using the FindControl method; however, most of the performance degradation is a result of a slow event firing mechanism. As you read on, you will see how you can reduce your dependency on the FindControl method by using a user control. Unfortunately, the performance won't improve significantly, but the code will be organized nicely and will be easier to understand and maintain.

Figure 5-6 shows the Web page, after it is created, using a repeater control and ItemDataBound event. You won't notice many changes in this screen except that we used the short date format this time for all date columns.

Order ID	Company Name	Last Name	First Name	Order Date	Required Date	Shipped Date
10248	Vins et alcools Chevalier	Buchanan	Steven	7/4/1996	8/1/1996	7/16/1996
10249	Toms Spezialitäten	Suyama	Michael	7/5/1996	8/16/1996	7/10/1996
10250	Hanari Carnes	Peacock	Margaret	7/8/1996	8/5/1996	7/12/1996
10251	Victuailles en stock	Leverling	Janet	7/8/1996	8/5/1996	7/15/1996
10252	Suprêmes délices	Peacock	Margaret	7/9/1996	8/6/1996	7/11/1996
10253	Hanari Carnes	Leverling	Janet	7/10/1996	7/24/1996	7/16/1996
10254	Chop-suey Chinese	Buchanan	Steven	7/11/1996	8/8/1996	7/23/1996
10255	Richter Supermarkt	Dodsworth	Anne	7/12/1996	8/9/1996	7/15/1996

Figure 5-6. Result of data binding by using an ItemDataBound event handler

Using Member Methods for Data Binding

This mechanism provides the best of both breeds. You can use this mechanism to control the content shown on the page declaratively, as well as use custom code to control the formatting options. This mechanism is similar to the inline formatting option except that you call a member method of the page class instead of the built-in DataBinder.Eval method. The member method is called once for each record that is being bound to the control. You can pass any input to the method according to your desire. In this example, we pass the current record being bound to the control by using the DataItem property of the Container object.

Listing 5-10 shows the HTML for using a member method in the data binding expression.

Listing 5-10. Calling a Member Method from the Data Binding Expression

```
<HTML>
    <body MS_POSITIONING="GridLayout">
    <form id="RepeaterWithMemberMethodDataBinding" method="post" runat="server">
<asp:Repeater id=CustomerRepeater runat="server">
```

```
<HeaderTemplate>
    <table>
        <tr bgcolor=lightgrey valign=top>
        <th>Order ID</th>
        <th>Company Name</th>
        <th>Last Name</th>
        <th>First Name</th>
        <th>Order Date</th>
        <th>Required Date</th>
        <th>Shipped Date</th>
        </tr>
</HeaderTemplate>
<ItemTemplate>
        <tr valign=top align=left>
        <td><%#ShowData(Container.DataItem, "OrderID")%></td>
        <td><%#ShowData(Container.DataItem, "CompanyName")%></td>
        <td><%#ShowData(Container.DataItem, "LastName")%></td>
        <td><%#ShowData(Container.DataItem, "FirstName")%></td>
        <td><%#ShowData(Container.DataItem, "OrderDate")%></td>
        <td><%#ShowData(Container.DataItem, "RequiredDate")%></td>
        <td><%#ShowData(Container.DataItem, "ShippedDate")%></td>
        </tr>
</ItemTemplate>
<FooterTemplate>
</table>
</FooterTemplate>
</asp:Repeater>
</form>
</body>
</HTML>
```

The ShowData method, shown in Listing 5-10, is a member method of the page class. This method needs to be declared as public so that it can be called declaratively from HTML. As shown in Listing 5-11, this method receives two parameters: the first parameter contains the record that is bound to the control, and the second parameter receives the name of the field that should be displayed on the screen. By using these two parameters, the ShowData method returns a valid value to be placed in the table cell field.

Listing 5-11. Code Example for the ShowData Method

```
public class RepeaterWithMemberMethodDataBinding : System.Web.UI.Page
{
    protected System.Web.UI.WebControls.Repeater CustomerRepeater;

    private void Page_Load(object sender, System.EventArgs e)
    {
        CustomerRepeater.DataSource = GetLargeDS().Tables[0].DefaultView;
        CustomerRepeater.DataBind();
    }

    public string ShowData(object Data, string ColumnName)
    {
        DataRowView inputData = Data as DataRowView;

        // Using the input column name to find the appropriate
        // cell in the input DataRowView object and return
        // its value. The date fields are formatted to show
        // short date string before returning it to the caller.
        switch (ColumnName)
        {
            case "OrderID":
                return inputData["OrderID"].ToString();
            case "CompanyName":
                return inputData["CompanyName"].ToString();
            case "LastName":
                return inputData["LastName"].ToString();
            case "FirstName":
                return inputData["FirstName"].ToString();
            case "OrderDate":
                DateTime OrderDate =
                    Convert.ToDateTime(inputData["OrderDate"].ToString());
                // Formatting to short date string before returning to the caller.
                return OrderDate.ToString("d");
            case "RequiredDate":
                DateTime RequiredDate =
                    Convert.ToDateTime(inputData["RequiredDate"].ToString());
                // Formatting to short date string before returning to the caller.
                return RequiredDate.ToString("d");
            case "ShippedDate":
                DateTime ShippedDate =
                    Convert.ToDateTime(inputData["ShippedDate"].ToString());
```

```
            // Formatting to short date string before returning to the caller.
            return ShippedDate.ToString("d");
        default:
            return "";
        }
    }
}

public DataSet GetLargeDS()
{
    DataSet MyDataSet = new DataSet();
    SqlDataAdapter MyAdapter = new SqlDataAdapter();

    SqlCommand MyCommand = new SqlCommand();
    MyCommand.Connection = new
SqlConnection(System.Configuration.ConfigurationSettings.AppSettings["n"]);
    MyAdapter.SelectCommand = MyCommand;

    MyCommand.Connection.Open();

    MyCommand.CommandText = " select top 100 Orders.OrderID," +
        " Customers.CompanyName, Employees.LastName," +
        " Employees.FirstName, Orders.OrderDate," +
        "Orders.RequiredDate, Orders.ShippedDate" +
        " from Orders, Customers, Employees" +
        " where Orders.CustomerID = Customers.CustomerID" +
        " and Orders.EmployeeID = Employees.EmployeeID";


    MyAdapter.Fill(MyDataSet, "OrderList");

    MyCommand.Connection.Close();
    MyCommand.Connection.Dispose();
    MyCommand.Dispose();

    return MyDataSet;
    }
}
```

The member method data binding mechanism shown in Listing 5-11 is much simpler than the event handler mechanism shown in Listing 5-9. We didn't need to use the FindControl method to find every single control contained in the repeater. We like this mechanism more than its two counterparts for a couple of reasons. The biggest reason is that it results in much cleaner code than its counterparts. We also like this mechanism because it provides the ability to use a real programming language to format the output to our desire. We are not limited by the format expression syntax that DataBinder.Eval can understand. We can even use this mechanism to compare the data-bound information with other fields on the page, data included in the view state, or even with the information stored in a database.

Another major benefit of using this mechanism is that it performs much better than the event handler mechanism. In fact, it performs just as fast as the inline format expression mechanism, as shown in Figure 5-7.

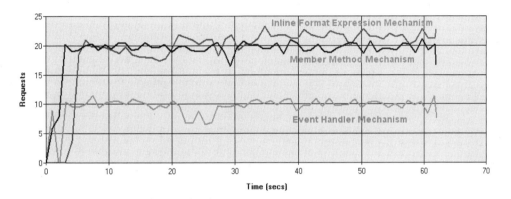

Figure 5-7. Performance comparsion between inline format expression, event handler, and member method mechanisms

Let's talk about how we can introduce a user control in our examples to clean the code and make it reusable.

Using User Controls Effectively

So far, we have used simple examples to illustrate displaying a list of records from the database. However, in many cases, the information that needs to be shown in a list is quite large and often reused across many Web pages. In such cases, we highly recommend that you use a custom-built user control to contain the reusable information. In this section, we will show you how you can carve the information that makes up an order record into a reusable user control and still use the member method mechanism to format the information during the data binding process.

We will continue to use the orders record example in Listing 5-12, but this example will use a user control to contain an order record. When the page is rendered, the repeater control will repeat this user control once for each order item.

Listing 5-12. Including a User Control in a Repeater Control

```
<%@ Register TagPrefix="uc1" TagName="Order" Src="OrderWithLabel.ascx" %>
<%@ Page language="c#"
Codebehind="RepeaterWithMemberMethodUserControlDataBinding.aspx.cs"
AutoEventWireup="false"
Inherits="ASPControls.RepeaterWithMemberMethodUserControlDataBinding" %>
<HTML>
    <body MS_POSITIONING="GridLayout">
    <form id="RepeaterWithMemberMethodDataBinding" method="post" runat="server">
        <asp:Repeater id=CustomerRepeater runat="server">
        <HeaderTemplate>
            <table>
            <tr bgcolor=lightgrey valign=top>
            <th>Order ID</th>
            <th>Company Name</th>
            <th>Last Name</th>
            <th>First Name</th>
            <th>Order Date</th>
            <th>Required Date</th>
            <th>Shipped Date</th>
            </tr>
        </HeaderTemplate>
    <ItemTemplate>
        <tr valign=top align=left>
        <uc1:Order DataSource='<%#Container.DataItem%>'
            id=MyOrderControl runat="server"></uc1:Order>
        </tr>
        </ItemTemplate>
    <FooterTemplate>
        </table>
    </FooterTemplate>
</asp:Repeater>
</form>
</body>
</HTML>
```

You can see in Listing 5-12 that the item template contains a user control called MyOrderControl. This control contains table cell HTML attributes to make up a complete order record. Because this control is placed in the repeater control, its value will be repeated for each item that is bound to the repeater. Notice how we call the DataSource property to provide the currently bound data row view object to the user control so that it can extract information and show it in table cells. The DataSource is a custom property that is defined in the user control. Let's look at the code for the user control in Listing 5-13.

Listing 5-13. HTML and C# Code Example for the Order User Control

```
<%@ Control Language="c#" AutoEventWireup="false"
Codebehind="OrderWithoutLabel.ascx.cs" Inherits="ASPControls.OrderWithoutLabel"
TargetSchema="http://schemas.microsoft.com/intellisense/ie5"%>

<td><%=OrderID%></td>
<td><%=CompanyName%></td>
<td><%=LastName%></td>
<td><%=FirstName%></td>
<td><%=OrderDate%></td>
<td><%=RequiredDate%></td>
   <td><%=ShippedDate%></td>

// Code behind for the Order user control.
public abstract class OrderWithoutLabel : System.Web.UI.UserControl
{
    public string OrderID;
    public string LastName;
    public string FirstName;
    public string OrderDate;
    public string RequiredDate;
    public string ShippedDate;
    public string CompanyName;

    public DataRowView DataSource
    {
        set
        {
            ShowData(value);
        }
    }

    private void Page_Load(object sender, System.EventArgs e)
    {
    }
```

```
private void ShowData(DataRowView inputData)
{
    OrderID = inputData["OrderID"].ToString();
    CompanyName = inputData["CompanyName"].ToString();
    LastName = inputData["LastName"].ToString();
    FirstName = inputData["FirstName"].ToString();

    DateTime OrderDateDT =
        Convert.ToDateTime(inputData["OrderDate"].ToString());
    DateTime RequiredDateDT =
        Convert.ToDateTime(inputData["RequiredDate"].ToString());

    DateTime ShippedDateDT =
        Convert.ToDateTime(inputData["ShippedDate"].ToString());

    OrderDate = OrderDateDT.ToString("d");
    RequiredDate = RequiredDateDT.ToString("d");
    ShippedDate = ShippedDateDT.ToString("d");
}
}
```

The DataSource property shown in Listing 5-13 forwards the call to the ShowData method, which uses the input DataRowView object to extract all necessary information and assigns it to member variables, such as FirstName and OrderDate. These member variables are accessed from the user control's HTML to populate text in the table cells.

The code behind for the Web page doesn't change at all. It simply contains the GetLargeDS method to retrieve 100 order records from the database and binds it to the repeater control as shown in Listing 5-14.

Listing 5-14. Code Behind for the Web Page That Contains a User Control in a Repeater

```
public class RepeaterWithMemberMethodUserControlDataBinding : System.Web.UI.Page
{
    protected System.Web.UI.WebControls.Repeater CustomerRepeater;

    private void Page_Load(object sender, System.EventArgs e)
    {
        CustomerRepeater.DataSource = GetLargeDS().Tables[0].DefaultView;
        CustomerRepeater.DataBind();
    }
```

```
    public DataSet GetLargeDS()
    {
        DataSet MyDataSet = new DataSet();
        SqlDataAdapter MyAdapter = new SqlDataAdapter();

        SqlCommand MyCommand = new SqlCommand();
        MyCommand.Connection = new
SqlConnection(System.Configuration.ConfigurationSettings.AppSettings["dsn"]);

        MyAdapter.SelectCommand = MyCommand;
        MyCommand.Connection.Open();
        MyCommand.CommandText = " select top 100 Orders.OrderID," +
            " Customers.CompanyName, Employees.LastName," +
            " Employees.FirstName, Orders.OrderDate," +
            "Orders.RequiredDate, Orders.ShippedDate" +
            " from Orders, Customers, Employees" +
            " where Orders.CustomerID = Customers.CustomerID" +
            " and Orders.EmployeeID = Employees.EmployeeID";

        MyAdapter.Fill(MyDataSet, "rderList");

        MyCommand.Connection.Close();
        MyCommand.Connection.Dispose();
        MyCommand.Dispose();

        return MyDataSet;

    }
}
```

When you execute the code examples shown in Listings 5-12, 5-13, and 5-14, you will see a Web page that shows a list of 100 orders. This Web page does not look any different than those shown in Figure 5-6. Though on the surface the page didn't have any changes, we used a completely different mechanism to construct this page.

BEST PRACTICE *The technique we introduced in this section takes advantage of combining a user control with the member method data binding. This technique can be very beneficial on large projects. The biggest benefit is code reusability. By extracting order information in a separate user control, we have made it possible to show the same information on many Web pages.*

This feature benefits Web applications that need to show different kinds of reports to their users. Many reporting applications reuse the same information for more than one report, making this technique a viable option. By using the member method data binding mechanism, we have simplified the process of showing data on the Web page while making it possible for us to use a real programming language to manipulate data if needed. Without putting such strong foundations in place, many programmers have found themselves limited by their own programming practices.

Imagine if we had used the inline formatting expression instead. It might work for the simple data formatting needs as shown in this chapter, but it would severely limit us if we wanted to perform more complex operations, such as comparing values with other controls or post-back information. It is important to build a strong foundation for your code so that you won't find yourself in a corner when you need to make adjustments later on.

Performance degrades with this technique because every instance of the user control needs to be instantiated, resulting in performance overhead. Our performance tests showed about 40 percent slowdown in performance when including a user control in any list management control, making it clear that the reusability comes with a cost. If your requirement is to maximize scalability, we showed you the performance gains from different list controls. To maximize code reusability and flexibility, we showed you how you can use a user control effectively. There is no golden rule to define when to use the user control mechanism. Every project has its own set of priorities, and we encourage you to evaluate your project goals and make informed decisions. Our goal is to provide you with the information you need to make such decisions.

Summary

This chapter focused on providing some very valuable and behind-the-scenes information so that you can make an informed decision about using list management controls. We hope that you have realized how data grid, data list, and repeater controls affect performance and that you will evaluate all three controls before picking one for your next project. We also hope that you have learned the inline formatting, event handler, and member method mechanisms of writing code to run during the data binding process. To emphasize code reusability and its effect on performance, we introduced the user control mechanism, which you can combine with either the event handler or the member method mechanism. Once again, we hope that you understand all this advice completely and are now better equipped to making appropriate decisions to satisfy your project needs.

CHAPTER 6

User Controls
and Server Controls

ONE OF ASP.NET'S great features is that you have a lot of choices about how to accomplish the various tasks involved in building a Web site. Unfortunately, without a good understanding of the various options, making the right choice can be quite difficult. One place we see people either struggling or making bad choices is with the controls they create for their Web sites.

It might seem from all the different control options out there that Microsoft had no better reason for creating them all than to confuse developers! However, there is a method to the madness, and in this chapter, we will talk about the pros and cons of each type of control that you can create to use in your Web sites—user controls and server controls—and how to choose the right one. In addition, we will talk about some of the best practices and traps involved with creating each type of control.

Choosing a Control Type

The biggest choice to make when working with controls is whether to create a user control or a server control. As we said before, there is some confusion about what differentiates these types of controls and why you should choose one over the other. We will first take an in-depth look at user controls, followed by a detailed discussion on server controls.

Working with User Controls

User controls are created and defined in the same way as an ASP.NET page or .aspx file. They include a design surface for laying out the HTML and client-side scripting. In addition, they provide the same mechanism as .aspx files for making declarations that affect processing such as caching. Each user control also has a code-behind file that defines the server-side processing for the control. The control lifecycle events are the same as those for the page class and therefore provide a familiar mechanism for working with the control. Think of user controls as mini-pages. They work almost exactly the same way except that a user control cannot be called directly through a URL; it must be contained in a page.

There are several benefits to using user controls. Because they provide the design surface and code-behind model, it is easy to lay out the design and behavior of the control quickly. And, because they are parsed and compiled just like pages, changes to the .ascx file are immediately picked up and included in new page requests without rebuilding the project.

One huge benefit to using user controls is that you can cache their resulting output, which is what Microsoft commonly refers to as "fragment caching" or "partial-page caching." It is extremely useful in situations where you might have dynamic content on the majority of the page but have something that is relatively static, like a list of categories or a high-level menu. Putting this portion of your page in a user control and caching it can be a huge performance benefit.

In Chapter 2, we discussed page-level caching and showed performance numbers for caching a page that showed data from a SQL database. The following example shows that with partial-page caching, we can realize these same benefits even if the entire page is not cached. Performance is also improved for a page for which only a portion of the page is cached, not the entire page. In addition, because you can use a user control on many pages, you can realize the benefits from using caching on every page in which the control exists, not just a single page.

Benefits of Partial-Page Caching

In the example presented in this section, we have built a simple set of pages that allow a user to browse the products in the Northwind database on a local SQL Server. The product listing page shows the categories of products on the left side, and, when the user selects a category, the products in that category appear. Clicking a product shows the user that product's product details page. The sample of the screen output in Figure 6-1 shows what the application does.

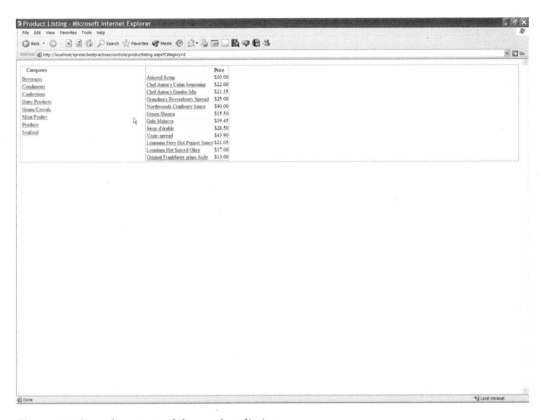

Figure 6-1. Sample output of the product listing

In this scenario, only the categories listed on the left will be cached. We could also use the page-caching mechanisms shown in Chapter 2, but the goal here is to show the benefits of partial-page caching. The Application Center Test (ACT) results displayed in Figure 6-2 show the difference among three different scenarios: 1) caching, 2) no caching, and 3) static category links defined in a user control.

Test Run Graph

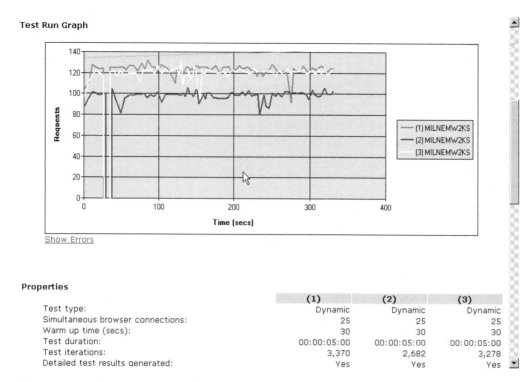

Show Errors

Properties

	(1)	(2)	(3)
Test type:	Dynamic	Dynamic	Dynamic
Simultaneous browser connections:	25	25	25
Warm up time (secs):	30	30	30
Test duration:	00:00:05:00	00:00:05:00	00:00:05:00
Test iterations:	3,370	2,682	3,278
Detailed test results generated:	Yes	Yes	Yes

Figure 6-2. Caching results

As you can see from the results, the static scenario performance is only slightly less than that when we used cached content. Keep in mind, however, that in this scenario, the database server is on the same server as the Web server and is processing only these requests. In a production environment where a greater load is being placed on the server, this separation would increase. The real difference comes when we compare the noncached version to either the static version or the cached version. The gains from simply caching this one part of the page are significant. These gains would be similarly increased as the load on the database server grew.

BEST PRACTICE   *Use partial-page caching whenever you can to gain the performance benefits it provides. Additionally, design your pages in such a way that you can separate static or semi-static content so that it can be cached. Do not put things, such as a time stamp, on your control that would keep you from caching it. Finally, you can create some dynamic content on the client that does not require server processing and that also allows for caching. For example, you can use JavaScript to display the current time and still allow your control content to be cached.*

Another benefit to user controls is that because they have a design surface and can be easily modified, if you design your page structure correctly and nest user controls, you can easily accommodate changes to the site. For example, if you have a user control that serves as the header for your pages, even if you don't use code behind, caching, or other features of these controls, you can make any changes to the header in one place and not have to change it on each page. This benefit is the only comparison to include files that we will make, but the goals of componentization that drive using include files is still a strong factor in working with controls.

There are some downsides to using user controls as well. First, because they involve a design page and a code behind, the code behind becomes compiled into the Web application assembly. This situation is fine if you are just using the control within the context of one application, but if you want to use it across many applications, this behavior is a bit of a problem. You can get around it simply by copying the .ascx file and the code-behind file into the new project and gaining some code reuse, but this is certainly not the best way to encapsulate functionality.

Second, though user controls provide a rich design surface for you to lay out the control, when they are included on the design surface of another control or a page, they appear as a gray box. This behavior makes it more difficult to plan around your control at design time because there is no indication of how the rendered control will appear in the page and affect other items around it.

Now that we have seen the benefits and drawbacks of user controls, let's turn our attention to the other type of control we want to discuss in this chapter: server controls.

Working with Server Controls

Server controls address the two major faults of user controls, which we described in the preceding section. Because server controls are completely contained within an assembly, they are easily shared across projects and can even be deployed to the global assembly cache (GAC) for maximum reuse across projects. They also provide a default design-time rendering of the control as well as the ability to customize this rendering so that these controls can be full participants in the design process.

In addition to addressing these faults, server controls also come with other helpful design-time features, such as being able to be added to the toolbox, providing interaction with the property browser, and being able to get information about other components on the design surface at design time. This last feature allows a given control to change or react based on the state of other controls on the page. Two powerful applications of this feature are controls that target other controls, such as the validation controls, and paired controls, which allow each control to stand on its own but also work with one another. An example of the latter situation might be one of the selection controls, like a drop-down list or radio button group that works on its own, which can perhaps provide some validation but can also be used with a special image control such that it can be configured to update the image when the options change.

The downside to server controls is that they do not provide any design surface to create the rendered display of the control itself. All the rendering logic for the control must be written in the .NET language of your choice. For simple controls, this issue is not huge, but if you need to create more complex controls, it can add a good deal of complexity and take a lot more effort to write the rendering logic.

On the other hand, because you use code to render your control, you actually also gain some benefits. For example, the Render method of controls, in which controls are responsible for putting their output on the response stream, receives an HtmlTextWriter object as a parameter. This parameter allows the Render method to receive classes derived from HtmlTextWriter that render tags appropriately for the given browser. Currently, an HtmlTextWriter32 class correctly renders tags for browsers that support HTML 3.2, which takes the burden off you as the control writer from having to deal with the nuances of browser differences for simple things like style attributes.

Now that you are familiar with some of the pros and cons of using user controls and server controls, we can turn our attention to answering the question of when to use one type of control over the other.

User Controls vs. Server Controls

Here are some simple rules to help you decide whether to use user controls or server controls when building a Web page:

Choose user controls when

- You want to take advantage of page caching for the output in the page.

- You are only going to use the control in one or two projects and you want to minimize development effort.

- You have a design team that will be responsible for making changes to the design and layout of the control, aside from just changing style sheet information.

- You are partitioning your page into smaller chunks to make it more manageable.

Choose server controls when

- You are designing for binary reuse rather than code reuse and want to encapsulate your control in an assembly. This might also be the case if you are planning to package your control and sell it.

- You want to provide page developers or designers with a rich design-time experience, including the ability to see how the control will render at runtime and at the application of styles and properties.

- You are targeting multiple browsers and want the built-in benefits of the HtmlTextWriter rendering, as well as full control over rendering your control, to account for differences in browser capabilities such as scripting support.

Now that you have an idea about what type of control to use, we can begin to look at the best practices to use with each type of control.

Best Practices with User Controls

It is easy to compare user controls with include files because they provide many of the same benefits. But to do so can really limit how you think of user controls and include them in your design. The first step to using user controls properly is to think of them as objects, just like any other class in your system, because they *are* objects, with properties, methods, events, support for inheritance, and everything else that comes with being an object. When you consider user controls as objects, many other best practices naturally follow.

Exposing Data to Subclasses, Containers, and Siblings

In thinking of your user control as an object, it is important to keep the inheritance hierarchy in mind. There are the basic inheritance issues, such as the fact that the class you define in your code behind will derive from UserControl, which will derive from Control. But it is also important to remember that your .ascx file will get compiled into a class that will derive from the class you create in your code behind. This relationship is important as you begin working with properties, events, and methods in your code behind, especially when deciding on an access level for them. Because your .ascx file will be compiled into a class derived from the one you create in the .cs file, it will have access to the protected members of that base class. This means that you can limit the scope of access for important fields and methods to be accessible only by those .ascx files that inherit from your code-behind class. For example, if you add a user control to a Visual Studio .NET project named MyUserControl, two files, MyUserControl.ascx and MyUserControl.cs, will be created. When the MyUserControl.ascx file is first accessed as part of a page, it will be compiled into a class that derives from the MyUserControl class defined in MyUserControl.cs.

BEST PRACTICE *Treat your user control as the full-fledged class that it is. Use proper encapsulation and expose data to subclasses and related classes only through strongly typed properties and methods.*

The example presented in Listing 6-1 is a simple reminder of encapsulation practices and inheritance rules and contains a Page and a user control. The user control contains code to fill a drop-down list with a list of items. This list is determined by the current second on the date time so that the number of items will be different each time the page is loaded. The control then exposes two different pieces of data. To its subclasses, it provides direct access to the ArrayList object that is used to populate the drop-down list. To other controls in the same container or its hosting page, it provides a public accessor to a private variable that holds only the count for the number of items in the ArrayList.

Listing 6-1. ProperEncapsulation.ascx.cs

```
public abstract class ProperEncapsulation : System.Web.UI.UserControl
{
protected System.Web.UI.WebControls.DropDownList DropDownList1;

    //Private variable only for this control.
    private int itemCount;

    //Public accessor for private variable (read only).
    public int ItemCount
    {
        get{return itemCount;}
    }

    //Protected variable for this control and derived classes.
    protected ArrayList seconds;

    private void Page_Load(object sender, System.EventArgs e)
    {
        seconds = new ArrayList(DateTime.Now.Second);
        itemCount = seconds.Capacity;
```

```
    for(int secondsIndex=1;secondsIndex<=itemCount; secondsIndex++)
    {
        seconds.Add(String.Format("00:{0:D2}", secondsIndex));
    }

    DropDownList1.DataSource = seconds;
    DataBind();
    }
}
```

With this setup, the .ascx file, because it derives from the class just listed, now has access to the "seconds" variable, which allows us to write code in the .ascx file that uses the seconds-protected member variable. Listing 6-2 shows a simple example of using that variable to get the number of items in the ArrayList.

Listing 6-2. ProperEncapsulation.ascx

```
<%@ Control Language="c#" AutoEventWireup="false"
Codebehind="ProperEncapsulation.ascx.cs"
Inherits="BP_Controls.ProperEncapsulation"
TargetSchema="http://schemas.microsoft.com/intellisense/ie5"%>
<asp:DropDownList id="DropDownList1" runat="server"></asp:DropDownList>
<br>
<br>
Total items in list: <%= seconds.Count %>
```

From the page that hosts the control, we still have access to the public properties but not the protected ones, so we can show the count on the page as well by using the method shown in Listing 6-3.

Listing 6-3. ProperEncapsulationHost.aspx

```
...
<form id="ProperEncapsulationHost" method="post" runat="server">
<uc1:ProperEncapsulation id="ProperEncapsulation1" runat="server">
</uc1:ProperEncapsulation>
    <br>
    <br>
    Page scope total items in user control: <%= ProperEncapsulation1.ItemCount %>
</form>
...
```

For many developers who are familiar with object-oriented development and design, this method may seem like common sense and not require an explanation in this book. However, we have seen many people struggle to understand how the different elements in ASP.NET interact and to be able to realize the true potential of an object-oriented Web environment because they forget simple things just like this.

Using Events to Communicate Between Controls

When you create your control, it is also important to realize that it will most likely be placed on a page with other controls, both server and user. This is important to think about because other controls may be interested in what your control is doing, and vice versa. Because you may not know ahead of time what other controls will be on the page, events provide a perfect mechanism to facilitate communication between your control and others.

A good example of where events make sense that we have used before is a user control that provides search functionality. We paired this user control with another control that was responsible for displaying search results. Both controls could be reused independently of the other. When we put these two controls on a page, the page was responsible for registering a method on the results control as a handler for the event raised by the search control. When the search was complete, the search control raised an event that passed the results of the search as a parameter to any registered handlers. The results control then received this data in its event handler and bound the data to a data grid.

Listing 6-4 shows how to use events to communicate between controls to make your control more flexible.

Listing 6-4. EventPublisher.ascx.cs

```
namespace BP_Controls
{
    using System;
    using System.Data;
    using System.Drawing;
    using System.Web;
    using System.Web.UI.WebControls;
    using System.Web.UI.HtmlControls;

    public abstract class EventPublisher : System.Web.UI.UserControl
    {
        protected System.Web.UI.WebControls.Button Button1;

        public event EventHandler ProcessingComplete;
```

```
        protected virtual void OnProcessingComplete()
        {
            if(ProcessingComplete != null)
            {
                ProcessingComplete(this, new System.EventArgs());
            }
        }

        private void Button1_Click(object sender, System.EventArgs e)
        {
            OnProcessingComplete();
        }
    }
}
```

This control contains a single button and exposes an event named ProcessingComplete. When the button is clicked, the event is raised. This is a pretty simple example, but it provides a means to show how events can help communication between controls. In this case, we are using the generic EventHandler delegate for the event, but most of the time, you will want a custom delegate because you will most likely be using custom event arguments to provide data about the event. Listing 6-5 shows the control that is notified when the ProcessingComplete event occurs.

Listing 6-5. EventSubscriber.ascx.cs

```
namespace BP_Controls
{
    using System;
    using System.Data;
    using System.Drawing;
    using System.Web;
    using System.Web.UI;
    using System.Web.UI.WebControls;
    using System.Web.UI.HtmlControls;

    public abstract class EventSubscriber : System.Web.UI.UserControl
    {
        protected System.Web.UI.WebControls.Label Label1;

        private void Page_Load(object sender, System.EventArgs e)
        {}
```

```
            public void Processing_Complete(object sender, System.EventArgs e)
            {
Label1.Text = String.Format("The control with ID {0} has completed processing",
    ((Control)sender).ID);


            }
        }
    }
```

This control does nothing unless its Processing_Complete method gets called. This method will get called when the event is raised from the publishing control (see Listing 6-6). To get this to happen, the two must be linked together. The page on which the controls reside is the best place to link them.

Listing 6-6. EventsInControls.aspx.cs

```
public class EventsInControls : System.Web.UI.Page
{
    protected EventPublisher EventPublisher1;
    protected EventSubscriber EventSubscriber1;

    private void Page_Load(object sender, System.EventArgs e)
    {
        EventPublisher1.ProcessingComplete += new
            System.EventHandler(EventSubscriber1.Processing_Complete);
    }
}
```

This simple page contains the two controls and wires the event handling method to the event. We first have to define variables for the two user controls because the Integrated Development Environment (IDE) does not automatically do it. We then have simply to use the Page_Load event handling method to hook the two up.

Now that the publishing control has defined this mechanism, any other page or control that is interested in knowing when the processing is complete can register as an event handler for this event and perform an action when it occurs.

BEST PRACTICE *Use events to allow user and server controls to both provide and receive information about what is happening on a given page. This loosely coupled communication mechanism is perfect for providing a means to communicate between disparate controls.*

Supporting Templates with User Controls

Another feature that is often ignored with user controls, but that can be very useful, is the template. Templates are often associated with server controls and are an important part of both the DataList and the Repeater controls. However, their usefulness is not limited to server controls.

A good example is the user control mentioned earlier that was responsible for displaying the results of a search. For this particular control, depending on the page on which the control was placed, specific content needed to be added to the control that gave disclaimers about the results, or tips for making sense of the results. This information couldn't be defined outside the control because it needed to be rendered among the other content for the control. A simple property on the user control would not work because we wanted the page to be able to supply some HTML declaratively in the designer so that the content could contain bulleted lists, bold text, or some other formatting. Templates, however, allow us to provide a means for the page designer to supply HTML content that will be rendered within our control. Templates allow our user controls to be more flexible because they are used across pages within our application.

The sample control in Listing 6-7 shows how providing support for templates in your user control can make it easier to use across pages and more flexible in design.

Listing 6-7. SupportTemplates.ascx

```
<%@ Control Language="c#" AutoEventWireup="false"
Codebehind="SupportTemplates.ascx.cs"
Inherits="BP_Controls.SupportTemplates"
TargetSchema="http://schemas.microsoft.com/intellisense/ie5"%>
<table>
    <tr>
        <td><asp:PlaceHolder id="headerContainer"
runat="server"></asp:PlaceHolder></td>
    </tr>
```

```
    <tr>
        <td>This is the static content that always appears on the
control.</td>
    </tr>
    <tr>
        <td><asp:PlaceHolder id="footerContainer"
runat="server"></asp:PlaceHolder></td>
    </tr>
</table>
```

The design surface for this control defines two placeholder controls that identify the location of where to put the content that the user specifies, which helps you, the developer, identify where you want the dynamic content and lets you put some constraints on it while still giving the consumer of the control the ability to customize it somewhat. Listing 6-8 shows the code behind for this control, including the definition of the template properties.

Listing 6-8. SupportTemplates.ascx.cs

```
public abstract class SupportTemplates : System.Web.UI.UserControl
{
    protected System.Web.UI.WebControls.PlaceHolder headerContainer;
    protected System.Web.UI.WebControls.PlaceHolder footerContainer;

    protected ITemplate _footerTemplate;
    protected ITemplate _headerTemplate;

    public ITemplate FooterTemplate
    {
        get{return _footerTemplate;}
        set{_footerTemplate = value;}
    }

    public ITemplate HeaderTemplate
    {
        get{return _headerTemplate;}
        set{_headerTemplate = value;}
    }

    private void Page_PreRender(object sender, System.EventArgs e)
    {
        if(_headerTemplate != null)
            _headerTemplate.InstantiateIn(headerContainer);
```

```
      if(_footerTemplate != null)
         _footerTemplate.InstantiateIn(footerContainer);
   }
}
```

In the code behind for the control, we simply create two properties of type ITemplate that correspond to the header and footer. In the PreRender event for the page, we check to see if any content has been specified for these placeholders. If content is present, we instantiate the templates in the placeholders we defined earlier. If there is no content, then it simply does not get displayed because the placeholder control does not provide a user interface. Listing 6-9 shows a page that uses this control and specifies content for the two templates.

Listing 6-9. TemplateControlHost.aspx

```
<%@ Page language="c#" Codebehind="TemplateControlHost.aspx.cs"
AutoEventWireup="false" Inherits="BP_Controls.TemplateControlHost" %>
<%@ Register TagPrefix="uc1" TagName="SupportTemplates"
Src="SupportTemplates.ascx" %>
<!DOCTYPE HTML PUBLIC "-//W3C//DTD HTML 4.0 Transitional//EN" >
<HTML>
    <HEAD>
        <title>TemplateControlHost</title>
    </HEAD>
    <body>
        <form id="TemplateControlHost" method="post" runat="server">
            <uc1:SupportTemplates id="SupportTemplates1" runat="server">
                <HeaderTemplate>
                    <b>Header Content</b>
                </HeaderTemplate>
                <FooterTemplate>
                    <i>Footer Content</i>
                </FooterTemplate>
            </uc1:SupportTemplates>
        </form>
    </body>
</HTML>
```

When the page renders, it contains the content specified in these templates and the static content that is always on the control. This technique is especially useful when you want to allow custom content in your control that is not directly before or after your control, but instead resides within the content of the control.

For example, many of the ASP.NET controls in the .NET framework contain an ItemTemplate property to allow the user to define custom layout for each item within the control.

BEST PRACTICE   *Use templates to allow part of the layout and design of your user control to be defined at the page level, which allows your control to be more flexible and still gives you all the benefits of having your code and user interface compartmentalized into the control. Do not forget that you can still take advantage of caching by using the VaryByControl attribute of the OutputCache directive to cache different versions of your control.*

Dynamically Loading User Controls

One feature of user controls that makes them attractive to many people is that they can be loaded dynamically from the file system. You can use the LoadControl method of the Page class to load a control from its associated .ascx file, which essentially serves the same purpose as including the control in the page, with one difference: the control is loaded and parsed each time the page is accessed, rather than only once when the page is first accessed. Using the LoadControl method certainly can provide a great deal of flexibility because you can determine at runtime which control to load and display, but be sure either to use caching or to do performance testing to determine the impact of using this method.

One large problem that we have seen people have with dynamically loading or creating controls is that handling an event from those controls becomes challenging. When a page posts back, the control that initiated the event must be present on the page to be notified that some action has occurred and to be able to raise its events. If the controls are being loaded dynamically, then the control that we previously loaded has to be loaded again so that it can react to any events. Then, after the events have been processed, the correct controls for the page have to be loaded, causing even more of a performance hit, as you have now loaded twice as many controls.

BEST PRACTICE   *If your user controls themselves or the controls they contain will be causing server-side events that you need to handle, do not load the user control dynamically.*

Though many of the same topics we just covered could be applied to server controls as well, some best practices apply specifically to server controls, and that is where we will turn our attention next.

Best Practices with Server Controls

Many people think of server controls as something that Microsoft or another third-party vendor develops and do not consider them for their own in-house development. This is a shame, because with a little bit of work, you can create a very powerful tool to use across your applications that easily integrates into Visual Studio .NET's design-time architecture. There are, of course, some pitfalls to avoid and some practices you should be sure to follow.

Raising and Handling Events in Server Controls

When creating server controls, it is important that you handle events carefully. There are two particular situations in which being careful is especially important. First, when you are making composite controls, you need to handle the events of contained controls. Second, when you are making a completely custom control, you need to be sure to raise appropriate events that make your control more valuable to the developers who are using it.

When working with composite controls, you have several decisions to make. First, are you going to expose the events of the controls contained within your control? If so, then you need to decide whether you will expose these events directly, expose custom events to encapsulate the events of the contained controls, or bubble those events up to parent controls.

If you expose the events directly, you are going to provide direct access to your child controls and let developers attach event handlers to the various controls' events. You can continue to encapsulate these controls and provide your own custom events, which you raise when events occur on your child controls. For example, you might raise the MyControlChanged event when the TextChanged event occurs on a contained TextBox control. This choice demands that you explicitly register event handlers for every event on the child controls that you plan to expose. If you plan to bubble events up to the containing control, then you can either bubble on those events that are bubbled from contained controls or register for events on contained controls and use the RaiseBubbleEvent method of the Control class to pass them up to the containing control.

Let us start by eliminating one of these options. If it isn't already clear, you should not use the first option. All rules of encapsulation aside, if you are building a server control that is a composite of other controls, you don't want to give developers direct access to the controls you are using in yours because you do not know what they will do with them and how that might affect your control's processing.

We recommend that you do the following:

- If your control raises events and you need, or think others might need, those events to bubble up to the containing control, then you should use the RaiseBubbleEvent method to raise those events. This method is especially useful if you have command-like events that are similar to those raised by buttons and link buttons.

- If you are building a composite control, be sure to override the OnBubbleEvent method and expose the appropriate bubbled events either as custom events or a generic event. As an example, the DataGrid control overrides OnBubbleEvent and raises specific events for Update, Edit, Select, etc. but raises the generic ItemEvent for any command event.

- Expose appropriate events for your control so that developers who use your control can appropriately interact with the process. For example, ItemCreated, ItemDataBound, and IndexChanged are all common events that many of the built-in controls provide. These events are provided because the developer might want or need to work with the item as it is being created or bound and might be interested in knowing when the state of the control changes. Be sure to let developers know when things are happening in your control and, where appropriate, how they affect the objects that are being operated on.

- Do not expose your contained controls when you are building a composite control. Either expose a similar event and register an event handler on your child control to know when to raise the related event or use event bubbling.

Design Time Experience with Server Controls

If you are going to take the time to create a server control, then you should make sure it integrates well into the designer surfaces in Visual Studio .NET. It does not take a lot of effort to provide a good design time experience for developers, and it makes your control easier to use, avoids headaches when your control looks different at runtime, and can speed development time by making it easier to configure your control.

At minimum, you should provide a design-time rendering of your control by creating a Control Designer class and assigning it to your control class with the DesignerAttribute class if the default rendering does not already provide a valid representation of your control based on the properties selected. Doing so will allow you to render some HTML to the design surface and use the properties of your component to do so in a way that allows developers to see the impact of their changes right away. Thus, if a developer changes a property that will impact how the control will render at runtime, the design-time rendering should show that, if possible.

If you want to go one further, then you can really provide a rich experience by making sure to add the appropriate attributes and create custom editors for the properties exposed by your control. Anything you can do to make the experience of developing with your control like that of the included controls will make it easier to use.

All this design-time work may seem like fluff, or something for control vendors, but think about how you would like to see controls act on the design surface when building an application. We like to know, without having to run our pages after every property change, what the control is going to look like at runtime. Knowing is especially important if you have designers who focus on look and feel, because the amount of time you will save them could be significant.

Additional Control Best Practices

Though server controls and user controls differ in many aspects, they also have a lot in common. After all, they are both derived from the Control class. This section covers some best practices that apply to both types of controls.

Using View State Sparingly but Effectively

View state is the persistence mechanism that allows a page to remember the state it held when it was rendered. It allows pages and controls to compare their previous state with their current state to be able to tell if anything changed. A hidden field is used to store the encoded data on the page, and the values are extracted on post-back and handed to the correct controls.

The process of encoding and message authentication checking (MAC) the view state is an expensive one. As we discussed in Chapter 2, the more you store in view state, the more of a performance hit you take both from the processing and from the extra network traffic needed to transfer all that data. Add a simple DataGrid to a page and then view the source to see how quickly view state can get out of hand.

That being said, view state is an extremely useful tool for the control developer. It allows you to store control-specific state information across requests so that your control can be more dynamic. For example, a good use of view state is to maintain a count of the items in the data source of a data bound control. On post-back, this count allows you to create the correct number of items for your collection so that they will be properly populated by the persisted data items.

Another good use of view state is to maintain values that are costly to retrieve. For example, if you have a page on which you provide a calculated value that is expensive to retrieve from the database, you might want to keep this value in view state so that you don't have to query the database again and force the value to be recalculated. You can accomplish this procedure in the Property Get and Set methods by using an indexed view state value to store and retrieve your data. You should always make sure that the data exists before you hand it back from your Property Get. This procedure is especially useful when you have multiple controls on the page and another control might cause the post-back. If your control's content was queried from a database or loaded in another event handler that will not get fired on that return trip, then you will lose your control values. Even if you can get them back with a database call, it is much better to hold onto them and simply display them again.

In the vein of being careful with view state, you should make sure that you are not duplicating efforts with other controls when you store information. For example, if you derive your control from one of the built- in controls, be sure you do not take on the responsibility of storing everything in view state if the base control will already take care of that. The last thing you want is to store the same information twice in view state. A good way to check whether you're storing the same information twice is to break into the debugger in the LoadViewState or SaveViewState method to see what else is there. You can also use the handy View State Decoder Utility created by Fritz Onion of DevelopMentor (http://www.develop.com/devresources/resourcedetail.aspx?type=t&id=827).

Using Client-Side Script with Controls

Another issue that often confuses people is how to reference server controls in client-side script. Because a control's ID attribute on the page can change based on whether or not it is contained in another control, many people end up getting script errors when trying to reference their control on the client.

The confusion occurs most often because there are several IDs that a given control has: ID, UniqueID, and ClientID. The ClientID property is the one that should be used when working in client-side script. Both this ID and the UniqueID include the names of each container control above the current control, thus providing a namespace for the control hierarchy, which is especially important for controls that render repeated items such as the DataGrid. The ClientID differs from the UniqueID only in the separators for the namespaces.

If you are building a script in the .aspx file and need an ID for a control, then you can use the following syntax to get this value:

```
var controlid = '<%= MyControl.ClientID %>';
```

Another frequent question is, "Where should we put our JavaScript?" One option is to put the script right in the user control or render it directly from the server control. You'll quickly realize the downside of this approach when two of your controls are placed on the same page. Now you have two instances of the client-side code in one page. Even if this doesn't cause your script to raise errors and get confused, it does add more network load to transfer all that script across the wire twice.

As we mentioned in Chapter 3, putting JavaScript code in a separate .js file and referencing that file is the best option for static script for several reasons. First, when JavaScript is in a separate file, that file is downloaded to the client and can be cached as a whole, which keeps you from having your JavaScript code go over the network with every page request. Additionally, you can make changes to the script file without having to recompile your controls or site when you need to make updates.

When talking about script in relation to controls, there is another reason to isolate your script: having multiple controls on one page, as we mentioned previously. Because your controls might exist more than once on a page, you can run into problems if you do not use good management techniques with your script code.

Use the built-in methods to register the script items that we discussed in Chapter 3. Doing so can keep you from rendering the same script twice in one page. When you use the built-in methods, if a script block is already registered with the same key, then the current request is ignored. Thus, the first registration of a script block always wins.

Indicating the Script File Version

Provide a version number in your script file and build your controls to that version. You should have a mechanism to check the version of the script file that is registered, which allows you to add a version to your script file along with your controls so that you do not break the interface between your control script and functions in the file. Doing so is extremely important because such a script does not provide a good environment for strongly typing or tying your code to a particular interface.

As an example, define a global version variable in your script file and put the same version number in your controls (a base control is a great place for defining this variable if you are sharing the script file across controls) as a constant variable. Then, when you render your control, render some script to validate that the correct version is present on the client and to raise an alert or exception message if it is not. Creating an alert allows you to know immediately that something is wrong and gives you the chance to correct it, rather than assuming or hoping that you have the correct script file working with the controls you are building. We'll show an example of this alert shortly.

Having multiple versions of script files lying around causes even more problems in that you need a good way to manage these various versions. Fortunately, there is already a place: the aspnet_client folder, which is installed in the root of the default Internet Information Server (IIS) Web site. Inside this folder is where you will find the JavaScript files for the validation controls and ASP.NET's smart navigation features. We recommend that you create subdirectories under this directory for your own JavaScript files as well. The structure is based on the company name, control or assembly name, and version. Thus, for a control, you might have a structure like the following:

```
Aspnet_client\APress\SuperTextBox\1.0\
```

If you are only developing controls in-house, then you can drop the company name if you like. Whether you use the aspnet_client folder or not, this method of organizing your script files is a good one. One key benefit it provides is that the script file for your control is accessible to any Web application on the server. Because the path to the file is based on the root of the site, you can have your control spit out the same reference on a page. There is no worrying about the relative path to your script file when you use this structure and use the path relative to the root of the site.

Listing 6-10 shows how to make sure your script version is correct for the control you are using. The first listing is the script file itself, which contains a variable that defines the version number and one simple function so you can make sure the script is working properly from your control.

Listing 6-10. SuperTextBoxScript.js

```javascript
var script_version = 1.0;

function SetBG(target)
{
    target.style.backgroundColor="Red";
}
```

The function defined here simply turns the background color of the passed item to red, showing that the script file was accessed correctly. Next, Listing 6-11 shows how we check for the correct version after registering the script file.

Listing 6-11. SuperTextBox.cs

```csharp
using System;
using System.Web.UI;
using System.Web.UI.WebControls;
using System.ComponentModel;
using System.Text;
```

```
namespace BP_Controls
{
    [DefaultProperty("Text"), ToolboxData("<{0}:SuperTextBox
        runat=server></{0}:SuperTextBox>")]
    public class SuperTextBox : System.Web.UI.WebControls.WebControl
    {
        private string text;

        [Bindable(true), Category("Appearance"), DefaultValue("")]
        public string Text
        {
            get{return text;}
            set{text = value;}
        }

        protected override void OnLoad(System.EventArgs e)
        {
            base.OnLoad(e);
            Page.RegisterClientScriptBlock("SuperTextBoxSupportScript", "<script
                src='/aspnet_client/supertextbox/1.0/supertextboxscript.js'
language=
                'javascript'></script>");
            Page.RegisterStartupScript("SuperTextBoxVersionCheck", "<script
                language='javascript'>if(typeof(script_version) == 'undefined' ||
                script_version != '1.0')\nalert('Script version must be 1.0');
                </script>");

        }

        protected override void Render(HtmlTextWriter output)
        {
            output.AddAttribute(HtmlTextWriterAttribute.Type,"text");
            output.AddAttribute(HtmlTextWriterAttribute.Value, text);
            output.AddAttribute("OnBlur", "SetBG(this);");
            output.RenderBeginTag(HtmlTextWriterTag.Input);
            output.RenderEndTag();
        }
    }
}
```

In the load event, we register two script blocks. The first is the location of the script file to support this control. Notice that we use the aspnet_client directory as a relative reference for our script file. The second is a startup script that checks for the version variable and makes sure it holds the correct value.

In the render method, a simple text box is rendered with an OnBlur attribute set to run the script function in the referenced script file. If there is a problem with the script file, we want to find it before this script runs, so we have registered the startup script to find any problems.

To test this method, load a page with the control on it and run it without putting the script file in the right place. You should get an alert window after the page has loaded, telling you that the correct version must be in place. To make sure that the code works as it should, create the following folder structure under the aspnet_client folder in your Web site's root directory:

```
SuperTextBox/1.0/
```

Copy the SuperTextBoxScript.js file into this directory and reload the page with the control on it. You should no longer receive an error, and if you enter and then exit the textbox, its background should turn red.

One last thing to keep in mind about the aspnet_client directory: it is installed only to the root of the default site. If you are running multiple sites on your server, then you need either to map a virtual directory on the secondary sites to the aspnet_client folder or to copy the folder over to those sites. We recommend the first approach, unless you are required to do otherwise, because it allows you to keep all the script in one place and not have to manage multiple copies of files.

Summary

In this chapter, we talked about some of the best practices and traps that developers often run into when working with user and server controls. There are performance differences as well as functional differences to be realized. Both types of controls provide a very strong model for developing, but you should choose wisely and use them to their fullest potential.

CHAPTER 7

Remoting and
Web Services

WITH .NET, CHOOSING a mechanism for making remote method calls is finally a positive experience. With .NET remoting and Web services, we have two great options. But with options come choices. One question we hear most often from developers is, "Microsoft keeps talking about Web services, but when should I use remoting?" Depending on whom you ask, you will probably get different answers.

There are at least two different camps when it comes to this topic. The first camp claims that Web services are the future of distributed programming and will be the only way to make remote procedure calls in the future. This camp looks forward to the new Microsoft Global XML Web Services Architecture (GXA) to provide improvements in security, transaction support, routing, and other services required for true distributed programming.

The other camp believes that there is certainly a place for Web services and looks forward to the improvements to come with GXA. But this camp believes that the true value in Web services comes in integrating disparate systems and platforms across networking boundaries, and that they will not be a panacea for all distributed programming needs. Remoting still has a strong place in this camp's toolbox for application development.

As you can imagine, the answers to the question first posed are shaped by those sentiments. The response of those who favor Web services goes something like this: "You should always default to using Web services and only use remoting when you need some service that is not currently implemented for Web services or you absolutely need the speed improvement." The response of the other camp is more along the lines of "Web services are great for interoperability and systems integration, but remoting provides the best performance and function for strict remote procedure calls."

We are sure you are asking, "So which camp is right?" But, before we get to that, we believe that it is always important to understand what factors are involved before making a decision. To that end, we want to lay out the differences and similarities between remoting and Web services and discuss where each is strongest.

Remoting Overview

In the .NET world, remoting gives you the most flexibility in how your remote method calls are carried out in a variety of ways: the options it provides for transport, serialization format, server host, activation, and state management are a few that come to mind immediately. With these choices, your configuration can go from mimicking Web services almost exactly to being completely contradictory to that model.

Transport

Remoting allows you to use either TCP or HTTP as your transport. HTTP, the same protocol used by Web services, is a more verbose protocol than TCP and is therefore slower. This flexibility is nice, however, because depending on the server host type you choose, you may want or need to use one or the other.

Serialization Format

When choosing which format to which your messages should get serialized, you have the option of using the Simple Object Access Protocol (SOAP), which again mimics the Web service world, or you can use a more compact binary serialization that improves performance. You can use these two options regardless of the host, and therefore it comes down to a decision between trying to use interoperability with SOAP or pure performance with binary.

Server Host

Remoting gives you the option of using any kind of Windows executable to host your server objects or Internet Information Server (IIS). Most often this means that you will be using either a Windows service or IIS in a production environment. Having this flexibility can be vitally important because some companies will want to limit the use of IIS on application servers due to its perceived security implications. Using a custom host executable, not IIS, is also the only way to employ the TCP transport to get the best performance.

Activation

Remoting provides for either server or client activation and supplies a rich lease management model for client-activated objects to control their lifetime. Allowing for different types of activation and lifetime management provides a distinct advantage for remoting in that it can adapt to the type of application that is using it. Distributed rich client applications can use client-activated objects and keep them alive to maintain state and provide a more "connected" application. Web applications can use server-activated objects to provide greater throughput and avoid object lifetime management.

State Management

Along with client-activated objects comes the ability to maintain state on the server for each client. Alternately, Singleton objects provide a means for keeping shared state on the server. With Web services, you have access to the same state mechanisms that exist for ASP.NET, including application state, session, and cache. For the session state to work, however, the client must support cookies, which not all do.

As you can see, the choices with remoting allow you to tailor your distributed application setup to the needs of the given application. You have a great number of choices with remoting that you do not have with Web services.

Web Services Overview

Unlike remoting, the Web service paradigm currently gives you fewer options. You must use HTTP as your transport, IIS as your host, and SOAP as your serialization format, and have server-activated, "single call" objects. However, the reason for this specification is because all these things are based on accepted standards of Web communication that many platforms and programming languages can easily work with.

The real power of Web services comes in the interoperability they provide. This interoperability occurs through using industry standard interface definitions (Web Service Description Language, or WSDL) and standard transport format (SOAP), as well as using the HTTP protocol for transport. Almost any platform today can host or call Web services; it is really just a matter of tool support. As long as the platform can send and receive HTTP messages and can parse a text stream, it can use Web services.

Tell Me Already! When Should I Use One or the Other?

All right, if you have not already guessed which camp we are in, then we will have to come right out and say it. Between remoting and Web services, remoting currently provides the most flexibility, the best performance, and the richest development environment of the two. For internal applications that do not require interoperability with another platform or application, remoting should be your first choice. Web services truly are the best thing to come along for application integration and should certainly be your first choice if you want to publish a service that others can consume or you want to communicate between disparate systems.

If your application will be primarily internal, but if you might need to integrate it with other systems, then use remoting as you build the application. When you need to publish the interface, create the Web service interface and use it to call the same objects you use in your application; you can even call remote objects.

That being said, Microsoft is putting most of its energy in this arena into Web services. With their Global XML Web Services Architecture (GXA) initiative, they are working with other vendors to create specifications for security, routing, transactions, and binary attachments, among other items. Microsoft is betting that these initiatives, along with their tool support, will provide for the richest mechanism of distributed programming.

Our feeling is that Microsoft will move all their services for distributed programming and the services just mentioned to leverage these specifications. So, even though remoting might be your best option for internal applications right now, it is vitally important that you get familiar with the new specifications and the tool support for Web services from Microsoft.

From an ASP.NET best practices perspective, remoting is usually the best choice for making remote calls, as performance is almost always a concern with Web applications. However, with updates and patches to ASP.NET and Web services, the performance differences are getting slimmer and may become insignificant. For beginning developers, getting started with Web services might also be a little easier than making a lot of decisions about transport, hosts, and activation types. The programming model and the tools to help you build Web services make getting up and running a simple process.

 BEST PRACTICE *Keep up with the latest work being done to extend Web services. The work that happens here will shape the future of not only Web services but remoting as well. If you do not know what is coming and plan for it as much as possible, your current design could lead to a good deal more rework in the future.*

Best Practices That Are Common to Remoting and Web Services

Once you have decided which technology, remoting or Web services, makes sense for your project, you still have a lot of decisions to make about which choice of technology could impact your project. The following sections present some general best practices that apply to both remoting and Web services.

Securing Your Remote Communication

In many applications, security is something that people try to add to their applications after the fact. Two big problems accompany this common but misguided practice. The first is that your application usually ends up being less secure than it should or could be because either you decide not to implement something after the fact because it would take too much rework or you miss a security hole because you did not design with security in mind. The other outcome is that you end up having to rework your design and, depending on what that means, you might have to rewrite parts of your application or deal with new constraints that impact things such as performance or scalability.

In planning your architecture for Web services or remoting, you need to consider two primary components of security. The first is securing the transmissions between the client and server applications, and the second is authenticating and authorizing the Web service or object consumers.

The first task is actually the easiest one for which to provide a solution. The first option, and the easiest to implement, is to use the built-in encryption capabilities of IIS by using Secure Sockets Layer (SSL). For Web services, using these capabilities is as simple as purchasing and installing a certificate on your server and requiring SSL for the virtual directory in which your service lives, which might mean that you need to separate your services from other application pages or services that do not need to be secured, though doing so is usually a minor deployment detail.

For remoting, the same setup is required in IIS, but you are now tied to using HTTPS as your transport. Your objects must be hosted in a virtual directory and SSL should be required for that directory. If you want to use a Windows service for your host, then you cannot take advantage of this built-in Web server feature.

Another option for both technologies is to write or buy a third-party filter that will encrypt and decrypt the data for you. This option is best suited for using an application internally because it requires quite a bit of administration and communication to implement across a network with many partners. With remoting, a channel sink that encrypts the data on the client and decrypts it on the server, and vice versa, would provide the type of security needed to protect your data. For Web services, you can use a SOAP extension to serve the same purpose. Again, in a Web services scenario, you would need some control over the client as well as the server to make this possible.

Keep in mind that encryption is only part of the story, and you might want to look into signing the messages as well. Encryption ensures that someone does not read the message while it is being transferred across the network, but it does not ensure that the message is from who you think it is from. To certify the message's sender, you would need to have the sender sign the message by using a hash of some sort or a certificate. Again, for this implementation to work in a highly distributed environment, you need a way to share a key value with the client to ensure whom the message was from, something that takes a bit more infrastructure to accomplish. IIS makes this a bit easier with its support for client certificates and the ability to map those certificates to user accounts, but it is still no small undertaking.

Yet another option, primarily for internal use, would be to use Internet Protocol Security (IPSec) to protect your data on the wire. Using IPSec is especially useful in a Web environment where you are communicating from your Web server to application or database servers and you want to secure that communication. Because this protection happens at the protocol level, you can use it with either technology. IPSec is included as part of Windows 2000 and can provide a good deal of security on all cross-machine communications in your environment.

Finally, for Web services, the emerging WS-Security (Web Services Security) proposal provides the means for encrypting and signing data within a SOAP message. The biggest benefit of this method is that it allows for only part of the message to be encrypted or signed, thus considerably reducing the overhead from encrypting the entire message. Because this method of protecting your data also relies on industry standards and is not platform-specific, it, along with SSL, provides the best option for the interoperability scenario.

For most applications, the easiest options internally are to use IPSec or to use SSL with IIS. Neither of these options requires any coding on the part of your developers and provides the most secure transport that has been tested and proven over time. Though the WS-Security initiative is promising and will eventually provide the best option for Web services security, it is still being developed, and tool support, though it exists for Microsoft .NET, is still a little way off. If you are currently developing Web services, keep your eye on the WS-Security initiative and plan your architecture so that you can take advantage of the tools and standards when they are ready. For more information on WS-Security, see `http://msdn.microsoft.com/ws-security/`.

 BEST PRACTICE   *Do not be lulled into a sense of complacency by using the binary transport for remoting. You should always use a true secure communications mechanism if you are transmitting sensitive data. Using prebuilt security technologies such as IPSec or SSL is almost always a better option than writing your own security.*

Performance

For sheer performance, using the binary serialization and TCP transport with remoting provides the best performance bar none, with approximately 1.5 times the throughput, according to some tests.[1] Small changes to this configuration for improved flexibility reduce your performance. For example, using IIS as a host and switching to the HTTP transport reduces your performance numbers a little bit, but it might be worthwhile for the added stability and flexibility. To add performance, you can add additional servers for little cost to scale your application.

Aside from the obvious choices mentioned previously, you can improve the performance of your remoting calls or Web service by using some of the following techniques and supporting mechanisms.

Caching

With Web applications, it is easily apparent that caching data on the Web server can greatly improve performance. You can apply this same mechanism to remoting and Web services. Where and how you cache data can have a big impact on your application's performance.

In most scenarios, you can cache data to one of two places: the client or the server. Web services and remoting are no different.

You can cache data on the server such that a return trip to the data source or expensive computation does not need to be performed. By caching data to the server, you reduce work on the server, which increases the throughput because the server can handle requests more quickly and therefore handle more requests. This practice works especially well for Web services and remoting scenarios in which the remote object returns data from a database or performs some expensive computation for the client. If the server can hold onto the data and not have to retrieve it, or can hold onto the result of the computation, then it saves the expense of performing these actions repeatedly. For example, a service that returns product prices would return data that does not change frequently. Therefore, the service could initially get the prices and cache them so that on later requests, the service could return data from the cache instead of making expensive calls to the database.

You can also cache data on the client, allowing for fewer round trips to the server. Caching data on the client improves performance on both the client and the server because the client can work without communicating directly with the server for a while and then post information back to the server if it needs to. A prime example of this situation is a client application that needs to work with some data and then update the database. Instead of constantly updating the database and dealing with the overhead of all that network traffic, the server

---

1 From the MSDN article "Performance Comparison: .NET Remoting vs. ASP.NET Web Services" (http://msdn.microsoft.com/webservices/building/frameworkandstudio/default.aspx?pull=/library/en-us/dnbda/html/bdadotnetarch14.asp)

can return a dataset to the client, which caches that data locally and works with it. After the client is done working with the data, making updates, deletions, and insertions, it sends the data back to the server in one call to update the database.

We have already covered caching in Chapter 2 and Chapter 6, so we won't show another code sample here. Suffice it to say that you can do server-based caching either declaratively by using the OutputCache directive or the CacheDuration property of the WebMethodAttribute, or imperatively by using the Cache object directly in your code.

Chunky Calls

One benefit of the client caching mechanism mentioned in the preceding section is that it reduces the number of calls to the server. Whether you are dealing with remoting or Web services, all calls to your remote object should be viewed as expensive. Even without caching, you can improve the performance of your application by reducing the number of calls you make to the server.

One easy way to create chunky calls is to plan your remoting objects and Web service methods accordingly. For remoting, objects that have a lot of properties that will be accessed on the client should be marshaled by value to the client so that each property access does not result in a network call. Use MarshalByRefObject on the server to return your MarshalByValue objects to the client.

Asynchronous Calls

You can make client applications at least seem to perform better by using asynchronous method calls. Even the most highly tuned Web service or remotable object involves some overhead in making the network call. In those cases where an immediate response is not needed or you would like the client to continue being able to work, asynchronous calls can be helpful. Listing 7-1 shows a client application making an asynchronous call to a remote object.

Listing 7-1. Asynchronous Remoting Call

```
//Asynchronous remote method call.
AsyncCallback RemoteCallback = new AsyncCallback(TheCallBack);
RemoteMethodDelegate remDelegate = new RemoteMethodDelegate(rof.GetRemoteObject);
IAsyncResult RemAr = remDelegate.BeginInvoke(RemoteCallback, null);

//Do other work here while the asynchronous method executes.
//Wait for the asynchronous method to finish.
RemAr.AsyncWaitHandle.WaitOne();
```

```
//Delegate for remote method.
public delegate IRemoteObject RemoteMethodDelegate();

//Method called when the asynchronous method is complete.
public static void TheCallBack(IAsyncResult result)
{
    RemoteMethodDelegate remDel =
        (RemoteMethodDelegate)((AsyncResult)result).AsyncDelegate;
    IRemoteObject output = remDel.EndInvoke(result);
    Console.WriteLine(output.Name);
}
```

The setup of a callback method, AsyncResult, and a delegate to invoke the remote method prepare the client application to make the remote call. Following the setup, the BeginInvoke method is called on the delegate, which initiates the remote call. We then use the wait handle after performing some work to wait until the asynchronous call has completed before moving on. The callback method gets called when the remote method is complete. In this case, we have combined two different mechanisms to get the result of the asynchronous method call: the AsyncCallback and the WaitHandle. Depending on your needs, you might choose to wait for the response by using the WaitHandle or let the callback method handle the response. If you do not need the result of the call to complete the flow of the current call, then the callback method may be more appropriate. In either case, your client code can continue to run while the remote code is running, improving the responsiveness of your client application.

 BEST PRACTICE *Use asynchronous calls where you can in your application to improve performance. Asynchronous calls are especially important when you have to execute several potentially lengthy calls. Use the methods shown here to help make asynchronous calls easy.*

Remoting Best Practices

Though there are many commonalities in approach when you are using remoting and Web services, each technology has its own quirks and unique issues. Both involve choices regarding the management of type information, yet each is unique in the mechanism used to manage those types and the best practices for each. This section covers some of the best practices specific to remoting, and the next section will focus on those issues that are unique to Web services.

Managing Types and Interfaces

When you work with remoting, one thing that always comes up is how to distribute the type information for your remoted objects to the client. This question becomes more complicated because only the interface of your MarshalByRefObject classes is required on the client, while the full code of your MarshalByValue objects must reside on the client. Because all calls to reference objects get passed to the server via the proxy, implementation code for these classes never has to leave the server. On the contrary, MarshalByValue objects get copied to the client, and all implementation logic runs on the client, so this logic must be present on the client.

You have essentially three options when dealing with MarshalByRef objects:

- Distribute the entire code for the object to the client (that is, just put a copy of the assembly on both the client and the server).

- Code to interfaces instead of classes and distribute only the interface definitions to the client.

- Create a metadata assembly by using the SoapSuds.exe tool found in the .NET Framework Software Development Kit (SDK) and distribute it on the client.

Each of these options has its advantages and disadvantages, as we will see.

The easiest of these three options to implement is the first: simply put a copy of your assembly on both the client and the server. You do not have to think about how you will distribute your classes into different assemblies. You do not have to worry about using interfaces in your design, and you do not have to deal with the SoapSuds.exe tool to try to get the correct metadata into an assembly.

The downside is that you now have your source code sitting on the client. For some developers, this may not be a big issue, but for others, this is a huge issue. Many companies do not want to deploy source code out on the demilitarized zone (DMZ) and want only presentation logic there. That is one of the big reasons for using remoting in the first place. For many of our clients, a typical architecture includes a Web server in a DMZ, a business object server behind the corporate firewall, and a database server behind yet another firewall. All access to corporate data is done by making remoting calls to the business object server, which can then access the database. All communications between the Web server and the business object server are secured with IPSec. In this scenario, the goal is to have on the Web server only code that relates to the user interface, keeping as much business-specific data out of the DMZ.

Another issue that comes up is when you try to debug or there is some question of whether you have remoting configured correctly. If all you have on the client is the metadata and your code is running, then you know the remoting link is happening. If there are any issues with your remoting setup, then you will know about them as soon as your code tries to access a remote object.

If you are already using interfaces in your code for all your MarhsalByRef objects, then the interfaces approach is probably the next in line in terms of ease of use. All this approach requires is that you define your interfaces in a separate assembly and distribute it to both the server and the client. This technique provides a nice separation of your code and ensures that remoting is set up correctly.

The downside to this approach is that you have to code a bit differently. Because you cannot directly create an interface, you have two choices: use the Activator class in your code to create the remote object, or use a Factory pattern to create the object and pass it back from the server.

In Listing 7-2, we access a remote object through its interface, allowing for the deployment of only the interface to the client machine.

Listing 7-2. Remoting with Interfaces

```
using System;
using System.Runtime.Remoting;
using SharedLibrary;

namespace Client
{
    class ClientApp
    {
        [STAThread]
        static void Main(string[] args)
        {
            IRemoteObject iro = (IRemoteObject)Activator.GetObject
                (typeof(IRemoteObject), "tcp://localhost:8085/RemoteObjects/
                RemoteImplementation.rem");

            Console.WriteLine(iro.Name);

            Console.WriteLine("Press 'Enter' to exit");
            Console.ReadLine();
        }
    }
}
```

The client indicates that it wants to get an IRemoteObject instance but provides the address of a remote object that implements this interface. In this situation, only the assembly that had defined IRemoteObject need live on the client. The assembly where the implementation is housed can be left on the server.

Instead of using the Activator class to get the interface, you can also use a Factory pattern to get remote objects from the server. In the code that follows, a remote object accessed through its proxy returns instances of remote objects that implement a shared interface:

```
BusinessObjectFactories.RemoteObjectFactory rof = new
    BusinessObjectFactories.RemoteObjectFactory();
IRemoteObject iro2 = rof.GetRemoteObject();
```

In this case, we create an instance of a remote object that is shared between the client and server, RemoteObjectFactory, and then use that class to get instances of the other remote classes that implement our shared interfaces. There is a bit more type information on the client in this case, but it makes it easier to have a flexible client that can be easily configured for remoting.

One way to make using the Activator class more flexible is to put the address of the remote classes in the configuration file and read them out at runtime. You still have to use the Activator class to instantiate objects instead of using the "new" operator, but with the address configurable, you don't lose the flexibility.

The final choice is to distribute only the metadata for your MarshalByRef objects to the client by using the SoapSuds.exe tool to create a metadata assembly. The biggest benefit here is that by using this tool, you can easily extract the metadata for the MarshalByRef classes in your assembly, which means that you do not have to plan your component model as carefully and you do not have to deploy the initial assembly to both machines, unless you have MarshalByValue types in the assembly as well. Because these types have to have their implementation on the client as well as on the server, the assembly would have to be deployed to the client.

To get around this issue, a little advanced planning will make this much easier. By putting your MarshalByRef objects in assemblies separate from your MarshalByValue objects, you can make the process simpler. In this setup, you can easily use the SoapSuds tool to create the metadata assembly for your MarshalByRef objects.

Choosing a Host

With .NET remoting, look to IIS as your host first. IIS is by far the easiest way to go for a remoting host. It provides for easier scalability, has built-in security features, provides application domain recycling, and has been thoroughly tested as a service. If you write your own Windows service (the only other real option for production use), you have to implement any of these items that you require.

If you really need or want the performance boost from using the TCP channel or you are restricted from having IIS on your application server, then you can use a Windows service that reads its remoting configuration from a file and simply publishes your objects. If you need your data to be secure, you can use IPSec or custom channel sinks, as mentioned previously. Once you start putting more functionality into your remoting host, however, the benefits are quickly outweighed by the ease with which you can use IIS.

One final thing to keep in mind with hosting is related to configuring a middle tier. A typical configuration file has a section for channels and simply references the HTTP or TCP channel as appropriate. However, if you have a middle tier host that both publishes and calls remote objects, then you might need to configure the client and server channels separately.

As an example, the configuration file in Listing 7-3 is typical for a host that publishes remote objects.

Listing 7-3. Simple Remoting Configuration

```
<configuration>
    <system.runtime.remoting>
        <application name="RemoteObjects">
            <service>
                <wellknown type="BusinessObjects.RemoteImplementation,
                    BusinessObjects"  mode="SingleCall"
                    objectUri="RemoteImplementation.rem" />
                <wellknown type="BusinessObjectFactories.RemoteObjectFactory,
                    BusinessObjectFactories" mode="SingleCall"
                    objectUri="RemoteObjectFactory.rem" />
            </service>
            <channels>
                <channel ref="tcp" port="8085" />
            </channels>
        </application>
    </system.runtime.remoting>
</configuration>
```

However, if you are in the situation that we just described where your application will be both a remoting host and client, then you will want to use something more like the code in Listing 7-4.

Listing 7-4. Remoting Middleman Configuration

```
<configuration>
    <system.runtime.remoting>
        <application name="RemoteObjects">
            <service>
                <wellknown type="BusinessObjects.RemoteImplementation,
                    BusinessObjects" mode="SingleCall"
                    objectUri="RemoteImplementation.rem" />
                <wellknown type="BusinessObjectFactories.RemoteObjectFactory,
                    BusinessObjectFactories" mode="SingleCall"
                    objectUri="RemoteObjectFactory.rem" />
            </service>
            <channels>
                <channel ref="tcp server" port="8085" />
                <channel ref="tcp client" port="8086" />
            </channels>
        </application>
    </system.runtime.remoting>
</configuration>
```

BEST PRACTICE   *IIS is the best first choice for a remoting host. It provides the quickest and easiest way to publish remote objects with all the necessary services such as security and stability. Start your design by using IIS as the host and then work away from it if you need to. For example, if you really need the performance of using binary serialization over TCP, start by determining if that need outweighs the work you may have to do to secure your remoting calls.*

Web Services Best Practices

Like remoting, managing type information is important with Web services. However, the issues are different because the way in which type information is used is different. The following section discusses some of the issues involved when working with Web services.

Managing WSDL on the Server and Service Locations on the Client

Like the type information for remoting, creating and deploying proxies used to make Web services calls is rife with trouble spots. The WSDL.exe tool is extremely flexible in how it creates the proxy for a Web service. Many command line parameters allow you to customize how the proxy works and is configured. Unfortunately, the tool support in Visual Studio .NET is not quite as good. You can change the namespace for the proxy once it is created, but you don't have much control after that.

The biggest factor in using this proxy is managing the URL for the service. Unfortunately, the tools in Visual Studio .NET hard-code the URL that is referenced when the reference is created. By using the WSDL.exe tool, you can specify that the URL should come from a configuration setting, which allows you to change the URL at a later date without having to recompile your proxy. In addition, the tool allows you to provide credentials for a proxy server and other information that may be necessary in all but a trivial operation.

The following command shows how to use the WSDL tool to create a proxy for a Web service that will get the address of the service from the configuration file for the application and the resulting proxy code that allows this retrieval to happen.

```
wsdl.exe /appsettingurlkey:UrlRoot /appsettingbaseurl:http://localhost/
    http://localhost/apress/webservices/mathservice.asmx?WSDL
```

Unfortunately, the parameters used in this scenario are not all that intuitive, so we will explain them here. The appSettingUrlKey parameter identifies the name of the key in the appSettings configuration section whose value serves as the root of the URL for the service. The appSettingBaseUrl parameter is used with the address of the WSDL file to figure out what portion of the URL will be hard-coded in the service proxy. In the preceding example, based on the appSettingBaseUrl parameter and the URL to the WSDL of the service, the hard-coded portion of the address will be apress/webservices/mathservice.asmx. The value from the configuration file will then be concatenated with this hard-coded path to provide the final path to the service. The code in Listing 7-5 shows the generated constructor for the proxy.

Listing 7-5. MathService Proxy That Uses Configuration

```
public MathService()
{
    string urlSetting = ConfigurationSettings.AppSettings["UrlRoot"];
    if ((urlSetting != null))
    {
        this.Url = string.Concat(urlSetting,
            "apress/webservices/mathservice.asmx");
    }
```

```
else
{
    this.Url - "http://localhost/apress/webservices/mathservice.asmx";
}
}
```

In this particular instance, we simply put the protocol and server name in the configuration file and left the relative path to the service alone. However, we just as easily could have used `http://localhost/APress/` for the appSettingBaseUrl parameter, in which case the hard-coded portion of the URL would be minimized to webservices/mathservice.asmx.

BEST PRACTICE   *When developing your service, use Visual Studio's built-in tools to reference your Web service and update your proxy. When your service is close to completion or you are ready to move into quality assurance or production, then drop the Web reference and create the proxy by using the WSDL tool. Either compile the proxy into an assembly and reference that, or include the proxy right in your project.*

During development, you do not want the hassle of having to recreate the proxy each time your service changes, and Visual Studio .NET makes it easy to update your reference. However, once the service is done, then the burden moves to the client when the service moves from environment to environment for testing and release.

Along with managing the URL on the client, the URL on the server is also important. The default and automatic behavior when requesting the WSDL for a service is that the endpoints defined in that WSDL use the server name that is used to request the WSDL. Thus, if we request the WSDL by using localhost for the server, then the endpoint defined in the WSDL will be localhost. This process works fine as long as your client and server are on the same machine, but move the client off the server, and you lose your Web service call.

The other reason to be aware of this last little tidbit is if you are giving the address of your WSDL file to partners or consumers. The endpoint address that is contained within that WSDL will be the URL that those partners use to call your service. Therefore, it is important that the address can be reached, but also that it gives you the flexibility you need to host your service. Therefore, the address should be a DNS name and not an IP address, which allows you to map the DNS name to whatever server you need to without the client having to recompile.

Summary

Remoting and Web services both provide a marked improvement in the area of remote method calls. And, though both can be complicated, they are infinitely easier to work with than the previous alternatives, like distributed COM (DCOM). The biggest challenge with both of these technologies is usually deciding which one to use. We hope that this chapter has provided some useful information that makes that decision easier for you. The next challenge that arises is managing type information, which we have also covered here. Deciding which technologies to use and how to configure them can be a challenge, but armed with the information in this chapter, you should be able to make those decisions more easily.

CHAPTER 8

Configuring ASP.NET Applications

CONFIGURATION HAS LONG BEEN a challenge in Web applications built on the Microsoft platform. One of the many improvements that ASP.NET brings to Web development is the XML configuration system. By replacing the registry, .ini files, and custom solutions, this new configuration system in ASP.NET provides a powerful, feature-rich mechanism to make your applications more flexible at runtime.

However, like anything powerful, if it's misused, the configuration system can work against you. This chapter focuses on the best practices to employ when working with the configuration system in ASP.NET. To take advantage of the system, you must understand how the system works behind the scenes.

Understanding the XML Configuration System

To understand how the XML configuration system works, it makes sense to start with a request for configuration information, such as that shown here:

```
IDictionary configValues =
    (IDictionary)ConfigurationSettings.GetConfig("MyConfig");
```

The first time that this or any configuration section is accessed in an application's lifetime, the XML configuration files are read and the configuration information cached in the application domain. This process seems pretty simple, but there is actually a lot going on in the reading of the configuration file.

The goal of the XML configuration system is to allow for easily editable configuration files that can be mapped into meaningful objects and values to be used in the code at runtime. To that end, each configuration section in a configuration file is mapped to a particular type that will handle the section and convert it into meaningful .NET classes for the application to consume.

This mapping of sections to handlers happens, where else, in the configuration file itself. The root element of an XML configuration file is the configuration element. The very next element is the configSections element, which contains entries for each XML element in the configuration file and the corresponding type that will handle it. Though you can technically place the configSections element in any configuration file, it is most often used in the machine.config file so that all applications can use the configuration section. A sample of this section from the machine.config file is shown in Listing 8-1.

Listing 8-1. Partial Machine.Config That Shows the configSections Section

```
<?xml version="1.0" encoding="utf-8"?>
<configuration>
  <configSections>
    <section name="system.diagnostics"
        type="System.Diagnostics.DiagnosticsConfigurationHandler, System,
        Version=1.0.3300.0, Culture=neutral, PublicKeyToken=b77a5c561934e089" />
    <section name="appSettings"
        type="System.Configuration.NameValueFileSectionHandler, System,
        Version=1.0.3300.0, Culture=neutral, PublicKeyToken=b77a5c561934e089" />
    <sectionGroup name="system.net">
      <section name="authenticationModules"
        type="System.Net.Configuration.NetAuthenticationModuleHandler, System,
        Version=1.0.3300.0, Culture=neutral, PublicKeyToken=b77a5c561934e089" />
      <section name="defaultProxy"
        type="System.Net.Configuration.DefaultProxyHandler, System,
        Version=1.0.3300.0, Culture=neutral, PublicKeyToken=b77a5c561934e089" />
      <section name="connectionManagement"
        type="System.Net.Configuration.ConnectionManagementHandler, System,
        Version=1.0.3300.0, Culture=neutral, PublicKeyToken=b77a5c561934e089" />
      <section name="webRequestModules"
        type="System.Net.Configuration.WebRequestModuleHandler, System,
        Version=1.0.3300.0, Culture=neutral, PublicKeyToken=b77a5c561934e089" />
    </sectionGroup>
...

</configuration>
```

Notice that the first two elements within the configSections element are Section elements that identify a particular configuration section that is to be mapped to the noted type. The configSections section must appear directly under the root Configuration element in the configuration file.

Next we see a sectionGroup element. The sectionGroup element is used to group a number of elements under one parent XML element. In the example, the System.Net group indicates that there will be a System.Net element under the root, which may contain the elements identified here. These elements, unless defined elsewhere, must be within the System.Net element in the configuration file if they are included.

When a configuration item is requested, the configuration system first reads through these identified handlers and stores the type information. It also reads through the actual configuration sections present in the configuration files and stores the element name for those sections, identifying them as "unevaluated." It does not, however, parse these sections until the application requests them, thereby saving processing time.

When a particular configuration section is requested, the appropriate XML element is read from the file(s), the type information stored earlier is used to create an instance of the handler for that section, and the XML element is passed to the handler for that section. The handler's responsibility is to generate an object that represents the XML element by using its Create method. The resulting object is stored in a static hash table and then handed back to the calling code. On subsequent requests, the configuration item is simply returned from the hash table, thus improving performance.

As an example, the first section handler we identified in Listing 8-1 was for the appSettings element. If we have an appSettings section in our configuration file as shown here, we can access that information as a NameValueCollection.

```
<configuration>
    <appSettings>
        <add key="mykey" value="some configuration value" />
    </appSettings>
</configuration>
```

Because the NameValueFileSectionHandler is defined in Listing 8-1 as being the handler for the appSettings section, it is passed the XML for the appSettings element and creates a NameValueCollection by using the "key" and "value" attributes from each add element. The next section will go into more detail on how to create these mappings and will provide some guidance for using them.

Identifying Configuration Sections and Handlers

Listing 8-2 shows two things. First, it provides another perspective on the configuration section information we just covered by creating a new configuration section and identifying its handler. Second, this example shows how to leverage an existing handler for new sections. In the previous section, we saw how to use the appSettings section, which is defined in the machine.config file by default. In this example, we see how to use the same configuration section handler on our own custom section.

Listing 8-2. Web.config with Custom Configuration Sections

```
<?xml version="1.0" encoding="utf-8" ?>
<configuration>
    <configSections>
        <section name="mailServers"
                type="System.Configuration.NameValueFileSectionHandler, System,
                Version=1.0.3300.0, Culture=neutral,
                PublicKeyToken=b77a5c561934e089" />
    </configSections>

    <mailServers>
        <add key="sales" value="sales.mycompany.com" />
        <add key="it" value="it.mycompany.com" />
    </mailServers>

  <system.web>
...
  </system.web>
</configuration>
```

In the web.config file, we have indicated to the runtime that there will be a custom section in the configuration file, and it will be contained in the XML element, mailServers. In addition, we have instructed the configuration system to use the pre-existing type NameValueFileSectionHandler to parse this configuration section and provide us with a .NET type that represents it. NameValueFileSectionHandler is the same type used for the special appSettings element.

Next, we added our configuration section, identifying it with the mailServers element and including "add" elements with a key and value for each mail server we might use in our application. This format is what the NameValueFileSectionHandler type expects to find in the configuration section it is handling.

The simple code-behind page in Listing 8-3 extracts the values from the configuration and displays them on a page.

Listing 8-3. Code Behind Reading from the Custom NameValue Configuration Section

```
using System;
using System.Collections;
using System.Collections.Specialized;
using System.ComponentModel;
using System.Data;
using System.Drawing;
using System.Web;
```

```
using System.Web.SessionState;
using System.Web.UI;
using System.Web.UI.WebControls;
using System.Web.UI.HtmlControls;

namespace WebConfiguration
{
    public class Example1 : System.Web.UI.Page
    {
        //Label controls for display.
        protected System.Web.UI.WebControls.Label key1name;
        protected System.Web.UI.WebControls.Label key1value;
        protected System.Web.UI.WebControls.Label key2name;
        protected System.Web.UI.WebControls.Label ErrorMessage;
        protected System.Web.UI.WebControls.Label key2value;

        private void Page_Load(object sender, System.EventArgs e)
        {
            //Get configuration information.
            NameValueCollection mailServers = (NameValueCollection)
                ConfigurationSettings.GetConfig("mailServers");

            //Make sure the configuration was retrieved.
            if(mailServers != null)
            {
                key1name.Text  = mailServers.GetKey(0);
                key2name.Text  = mailServers.GetKey(1);

                key1value.Text = mailServers.GetValues(0)[0];
                key2value.Text = mailServers.GetValues(1)[0];
            }
            else
                ErrorMessage.Visible = true;
        }
    }
}
```

As you can see, we simply get the configuration section by calling GetConfig and then make sure it is not null. If it is not null, then we display the keys and values that we know are in the file. We now have a custom configuration section without having to write any code to deal with converting from XML to a .NET type. We have also created a custom configuration section that now has more meaning than appSettings and calls out more specifically what this information relates to.

 BEST PRACTICE *Always check to make sure that the configuration is not null. Your application should fail gracefully or handle missing configuration information in case someone changes it. If the configuration information is needed for your application, show a custom error message that indicates that the application is not configured correctly so that an administrator can quickly fix the problem.*

The outcome of our example from Listing 8-2 and Listing 8-3 is shown in Figure 8-1.

Figure 8-1. Output from simple configuration settings

Leveraging the Built-In Configuration Handlers

Microsoft has already taken the time to develop many configuration section handlers. Some of these handlers are very domain-specific, such as the handlers that work with the remoting configuration data, while others are more generic, such as NameValueFileSectionHandler, which we used in the last example. These more generic handlers can be very convenient and can often be used for many of your configuration tasks.

 BEST PRACTICE *Leverage the built-in types in the .NET framework to handle your configuration when it makes sense. Doing so saves you the time and effort in creating the handler as well as, and probably more importantly, the time involved in testing and working out bugs.*

The three most helpful built-in handlers are listed in Table 8-1.

Table 8-1. Helpful Built-In Configuration Section Handlers

TYPE	DESCRIPTION	RETURNED TYPE
SingleTagSectionHandler	Handles a single XML element with attributes.	IDictionary
NameValueSectionHandler	Handles key value pairs by using the "add" element and the key and value attributes.	NameValueCollection
DictionarySectionHandler	Handles key value pairs by using the "add" element and the key and value attributes.	HashTable

The first thing to notice about this list of handlers is that NameValueSectionHandler and the DictionarySectionHandler appear to do the same thing. Although these two handlers do both handle the same type of configuration sections, they store the information in different collection types to support different needs. There are numerous types of collections in the .NET framework, and each has its strong and weak points. Depending on how you are going to use the information in the configuration file or what you are storing there, you may want a different collection type for your information. With these two handlers, you have two options right out of the box.

The second thing to notice in Table 8-1 is that the NameValueFileSectionHandler class used earlier is not present, which is because NameValueFileSectionHandler is not part of the public interface for the .NET framework. If you look for this type in your Microsoft Developer Network help, you will find it listed, but it is marked as supporting the .NET infrastructure. The question then becomes, should you use it? That question is one that is best answered in the context of a given project. Because this is not a part of the public interface, there is a level of risk. However, rather than allowing you to ponder this question all day, we have simply included a handler in the sample code for this chapter that provides the same functionality, for Web applications only, with full source so that the risk is removed. What does this handler do that it is so worth having? The next section shows exactly how powerful this handler can be.

NOTE   *Though NameValueSectionHandler is not part of the public API for the .NET framework, Microsoft has encouraged users to take advantage of the handler's functionality as it applies to the appSettings element in the configuration file. Several articles and white papers offer tips similar to those in the next section, but they only apply to the AppSettings property of the ConfigurationSettings class to access settings.*

User- or Environment-Specific Settings

There is a little known feature of the appSettings section that is extremely useful. The appSettings XML element can have an attribute named "file" that points to a separate file that contains only an appSettings section. If this file is present, the values in that file are included in the returned collection. In addition, if an item is present in that file and the web.config file, the one from the external file will be used instead.

Why is this so useful? This feature makes life much easier in several areas. In development scenarios where the source code is under source control, it makes sense to have the web.config retain its values for things like database servers and other settings that may differ in different environments. Two examples of these scenarios would be a developer who wants to configure his or her environment to point to a local database for debugging instead of at a shared database, and the case where the database server is different for the developer, QA, and production. NameValueFileSectionHandler, used to read the appSettings section, allows for these types of situations.

In the following example, we extend the example from Listings 8-2 and 8-3 by leveraging the capabilities of NameValueFileSectionHandler so that the email servers we are referencing in production can stay in the web.config file but the servers we want to use during development are in a separate file.

The web.config file that appears in Listing 8-4 looks the same as it did before, except that we have added the "file" attribute to the section element to indicate that other settings, or overrides, can be found in the devsettings.config file. In addition, we have created a devsettings.config file, shown in Listing 8-5 a little later, which contains our development settings.

Listing 8-4. Configuration File That Uses the "file" Attribute of NameValueFileSectionHandler

```
<?xml version="1.0" encoding="utf-8" ?>
<configuration>
    <configSections>
     <section name="mailServers"
type="System.Configuration.NameValueFileSectionHandler, System,
Version=1.0.3300.0, Culture=neutral, PublicKeyToken=b77a5c561934e089" />
    </configSections>

    <mailServers file="devsettings.config">
     <add key="sales" value="sales.mycompany.com" />
     <add key="it" value="it.mycompany.com" />
    </mailServers>
```

```
<system.web>
    ...
</system.web>
</configuration>
```

This configuration indicates that there are other settings in the devsettings.config file that should also be applied to the setup (see Listing 8-5). In this separate file for developer settings, we will redefine the "it" server name and add the marketing server. In reality, you probably will not add new elements to this file, but that depends on how you leverage this handler's capabilities. We show it here primarily to demonstrate that this section is handled much the same way that a child configuration section is handled, which we will cover in the upcoming "Cascading Configuration" section.

Listing 8-5. Settings in the devsettings.config File

```
<mailServers>
    <add key="marketing" value="devmarketing.mycompany.com" />
    <add key="it" value="devit.mycompany.com" />
</mailServers>
```

As you can see in Figure 8-2, the settings from our special file are now included when we use the code from Listing 8-3 to retrieve the values from our configuration file.

Figure 8-2. User-specific settings

There are several things to keep in mind when working with this handler or this type of setup. First, ASP.NET will not pick up changes to the external file at runtime. Only when the application domain starts will it pick up changes to this file. More details on how ASP.NET allows for dynamically changing configuration are included in the section "Application Domains and Automatic Reloading of Configuration Settings," later in this chapter. Suffice it to say that if you use this mechanism, you will either have to change something in your web.config as well or restart IIS to get your application to reload and pick up the changes to this file.

Second, when using source control, you should not store user-specific settings in the source control system, or at least not with the same project. Separate these settings from your code because they only make sense in a given context. Because these settings are user-specific, it does not make sense to put them under source control. If everyone is going to use the same file, then you should just put the settings right in the web.config file.

Along those same lines, you should not include the user- or environment-specific files as part of your project. They can reside in the file folder with your other project files but should not appear as part of your Web application project in Visual Studio .NET. If you need to see the file in the solution explorer, simply select your project in the solution explorer and click the Show All Files button. You can then see your file and double-click it to open it, but it won't be an actual part of your project. Because at deployment time you do not want these files to go out, you do not want Visual Studio .NET to consider them part of your project. Many build and deployment tools will use the solution file to determine what files should be included.

BEST PRACTICE   *Do use the NameValueFileSectionHandler capabilities, either through the built-in appSettings section, directly using the NameValueFileSectionHandler class, or through a custom class similar to the one included in the code download for this chapter at http://www.apress.com/. Make the default web.config settings the same as your production settings so that the values will be right when you deploy your application to production. It is better to have to troubleshoot configuration issues in QA or development.*

Do not deploy the user-specific settings files along with the main web.config to production or any environment where the defaults should be used. If the file referenced in the appSettings elements is not found, then those values are not included in the configuration information, and no exception is thrown.

Do not rely on ASP.NET to pick up changes to the supplementary configuration document during runtime.

Do not include the user- or environment-specific settings files in your project or in source control.

Application Domains and Automatic Reloading of Configuration Settings

ASP.NET adds a special capability to the configuration system that standard .NET applications do not have: dynamic reloading of configuration information. What this means is that in ASP.NET applications, changes to the configuration file are picked up immediately so that new requests for configuration information will receive any updated information.

At the time that a Web application is initialized, ASP.NET adds file dependencies and sets watchers for these files so that any changes to the files can be monitored. This process is how the runtime can notice changes to .aspx files in your Web application and recompile those pages on the fly. Likewise, changes to the configuration file for a Web application can be caught and the configuration information updated to allow the new values to be seen by an application.

Figures 8-3 and 8-4 show this practice in action. Figure 8-3 shows our sample application from Listings 8-2 and 8-3 with two values from the configuration section. Figure 8-4 shows the same page after changing the "sales" entry, saving the configuration file, and then refreshing the Web page. Notice that the value of the server name for the sales entry has changed.

Figure 8-3. Before updating the configuration file

Figure 8-4. After updating the configuration file

Naturally, costs are associated with this flexibility. To be able to update the configuration information that is already stored in the application domain, a new application domain must be created and the Web application must be loaded into this new domain. So, while the new changes are picked up, any information that was previously in memory now needs to be reloaded from the configuration files as well, which means that we have invalidated our cache of configuration data. Notice in Figures 8-3 and 8-4 that the name of the application domain is shown below the configuration information. The numeral after the name of the application increased from 7 to 8 when we changed the configuration file, showing that our code is now running in a new application domain.

Obviously, you would not want this to happen often for many reasons. One good example is that any InProcess session data and cache entries that you accumulated would be discarded, along with the old application domain, because the cache is kept at an application domain level and the InProcess session is stored in the cache.

BEST PRACTICE *Do not set up a system in which the configuration information will change. Information in the configuration files should be fairly static and change primarily with deployments.*

If you will be changing configuration files as part of a deployment or otherwise, store this information in an external XML file and cache the values yourself. As discussed in Chapter 2, you can easily add file dependencies to your cache items so that if your XML file changes, you will be able to reload that custom configuration.

Cascading Configuration

In the discussion of user-specific settings, we mentioned the notion of multiple configuration files and "cascading" configuration data. Cascading configuration data is another powerful feature of the .NET configuration system that, though all applications can take advantage of it, is even more powerful in the context of ASP.NET.

In general, when working with or accessing configuration information for an application, ASP.NET actually consults many configuration files. At minimum, the machine.config file is read, and if the application has a configuration file, then that is also read. In addition, items in the enterprise.config, security.config ,and user.config files also get included in the application's configuration. Generally speaking, these latter three files are used to apply security settings to application domains and are not used for configuring the applications themselves.

In an ASP.NET Web site, the machine.config and web.config files are merged together to provide a single set of configuration data for the application, which means that when querying the configuration system, the developer does not need to worry about whether a section is defined in the machine.config file or the web.config file, as both will be consulted to find the requested configuration. Items that are defined at a higher level can be overridden at a lower level simply by being redefined.

In the ASP.NET world, the added bonus is that web.config files also cascade. You can define information in a web.config file at the root of your site or in a root virtual directory and have that information available to all the applications in that directory. The benefit is that you can put common configuration information in one place, rather than put a copy of it in each application. Additionally, you can put global Web settings in the main root, rather than having to update the machine.config file to include application-specific settings.

The first question many people have when they hear this is, "What if I want to keep people from overriding those settings?" For example, what if you want to enter a setting in the root web.config and want to make sure that that value is the same for all applications? No subapplication should be able to change that configuration data. To handle this situation in a Web application, you can use the Location element, which allows you to provide a path, some configuration information, and an attribute to indicate if the information is allowed to be overridden.

Listing 8-6 shows both how to leverage the cascading configuration as well as how to lock down configuration sections so that they cannot be overridden in

an application. We start by creating a web.config file to put in the root of our
Web site.

Listing 8-6. web.config (Root)

```
<?xml version="1.0" encoding="utf-8" ?>
<configuration>

    <configSections>
            <section name="mailServers"
type="System.Configuration.NameValueFileSectionHandler, System,
Version=1.0.3300.0, Culture=neutral,
PublicKeyToken=b77a5c561934e089"
allowDefinition="MachineToApplication"/>
        </configSections>

    <mailServers>
            <add key="sales" value="sales.mycompany.com" />
        </mailServers>

</configuration>
```

This listing should look familiar because it is similar to the configuration
files we have been working with at the application level. We simply identified
the section and then entered a single value for the "sales" mail server. The
web.config code for the application now looks a bit different, however, as shown
in Listing 8-7.

Listing 8-7. web.config (Application)

```
<?xml version="1.0" encoding="utf-8" ?>
<configuration>

    <mailServers>
            <add key="it" value="it.mycompany.com" />
        </mailServers>

  <system.web>
...
  </system.web>
</configuration>
```

Notice that we no longer have the configSections element to indicate the handler for our custom section, as this is defined in the root web.config file. This is a nice way to make your handlers available to all your Web applications. Keep in mind that your applications will have to be able to find the handler for the section. In this case, the assembly that contains the handler resides in the Global Assembly Cache, and so it is available to all applications.

In addition, we have only one value specified in the mailServers section for the IT department's mail server. If we run our same Web page again, we get the same results as if we had defined these two values in the same configuration file. The resulting output is exactly like that shown earlier in Figure 8-1.

Another important fact to keep in mind with this type of configuration is that for the section handlers included in the .NET framework, values with the same name or key defined at a lower level will overwrite values from a higher level directory. For example, if we also add a "sales" entry to the web.config at the application level but with a different value than the entry in the web.config located at the root of the site, we see that the value in the application file is used (see Listing 8-8).

Listing 8-8. web.config (Updated Application)

```xml
<?xml version="1.0" encoding="utf-8" ?>
<configuration>

    <mailServers>
    <add key="sales" value="sales.mycompany.com" />
    <add key="it" value="it.mycompany.com" />
    </mailServers>

  <system.web>
...
  </system.web>
</configuration>
```

The new value of sales.mycompany.com is now retrieved from the file closest to the application, as it has overridden the parent value. In many cases, this behavior is exactly what we want to have happen. It works very well to provide a default value but allows for a given application to use a new value, which provides maximum flexibility. But if we want maximum conformance, then we can lock down the settings. By simply wrapping the section in the root web.config file with a location element that specifies false for the allowOverride attribute, we can indicate that no subdirectory or application should be able to override the settings (see Listing 8-9).

Listing 8-9. web.config (Root Updated)

```
<?xml version="1.0" encoding="utf-8" ?>
<configuration>
    <configSections>
        <section name="mailServers"
type="System.Configuration.NameValueFileSectionHandler, System,
Version=1.0.3300.0, Culture=neutral,
PublicKeyToken=b77a5c561934e089"
allowDefinition="MachineToApplication"/>
    </configSections>

<location path="." allowOverride="false">
    <mailServers>
        <add key="sales" value="salesmail.mycompany.com" />
    </mailServers>
</location>

</configuration>
```

By adding the location element and specifying the path to be equal to ".", we essentially have said that the configuration information included within this Location element should be applied to all directories included below the current one. In addition, we have set allowOverride to false, indicating that any application in the path specified, all of them in our case, should not be able to redefine this section in their own configuration files and will be forced to use these settings when querying the included configuration sections.

After applying the changes, if we try to run our page again, we get a configuration exception that tells us that this section has been locked down and cannot be redefined (see Figure 8-5).

One other mechanism for restricting where items can be defined is to use the allowDefinition attribute on the "section" element when registering the handler for a section. This attribute takes one of three values: Everywhere, MachineToApplication, or MachineOnly. The first two allow the configuration information to be defined at lower levels, while the latter only allows sections to be defined in the machine.config file. The values will continue to cascade down and be available to the Web applications, but they cannot be redefined. Using this mechanism allows for the same restriction as our use of the location element in Listing 8-9, with the added benefit that it allows other applications on the machine, and not just ASP.NET applications, to use this configuration section. However, the allowDefinition attribute applies only to ASP.NET applications, which means that other types of applications would be able to override this configuration. The location tag is only used by ASP.NET, and other applications cannot read the information found in the location element. Therefore, if you have a configuration that you need to share across Web applications, client executables, or services, do not use the location element; rather, use the allowDefinition attribute.

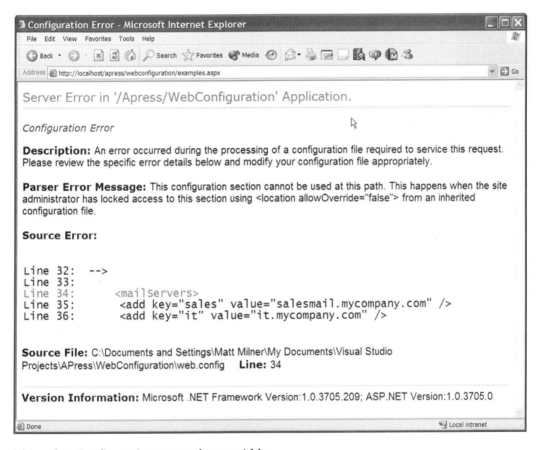

Figure 8-5. Configuration cannot be overridden

BEST PRACTICE *Do use the cascading configuration to your bene-fit by defining shared information at a higher level, either site root or in the machine.config.*

Logically separate your configuration settings into their own sections, even if they use the same handler. Do not just use the appSettings section as a catch-all for your settings. The benefit of this practice is twofold. First, because your information is logically organized, it makes more sense to someone working on or review-ing your application. Second, because your information is segregated, if need be, different sections can be locked down at a given level so that they cannot be redefined. If you have only one section, then you have to lock down all settings at the higher level. An example would be to group mail servers or database servers together or define other machine addresses that are used together.

> *Do take advantage of the Location element. It comes in handy not only when you want to lock down a section of your configuration, but also when you want to apply configuration selectively to a particular subdirectory or file from within an application. For example, you could either require or ignore authentication for a given file or directory so that the security for that item would be different than on the other items.*
>
> *Do use the allowDefinition attribute on your section definitions to make explicit how this section should be used.*

Creating Custom Configuration Section Handlers

This last section is about the best practices to use when building a configuration section handler of your own. When the built-in handlers will not meet your needs, it is time to build your own handler. It is not a difficult task, but it is important that you make sure that your handler will work as expected in the ASP.NET world.

The sample handler we will build in this section will be similar to NameValueSectionHandler we discussed earlier, with one major exception: we will encrypt the values in our config file. The job of the handler will be to decrypt the value and pass back a string value for the given key. One major problem with the configuration system in the .NET framework is the fact that things are in clear text on the hard drive and, in the case of ASP.NET, in the virtual directory. Though measures are taken to ensure that your web.config is not downloaded by a malicious user, we recommend that you use extra caution when storing anything important in the web.config. An easy example is database connection strings. Usually, applications use a specific user name and password to connect to a database in order to take advantage of ADO.NET connection pooling. It is not a good practice to have these credentials lying around in clear text. Luckily, .NET makes encrypting and decrypting strings very easy.

 BEST PRACTICE *Never put unencrypted credentials in a web.config file. Even in the machine.config, these items are not as safe as they should be. If a user gets access to your Web server in the DMZ, you want to limit the access they have to the other resources in your network as much as possible.*

Before we get started, there are several things that we want to be sure our handler does so that it plays well with others in the .NET environment. First, we need to allow for cascading of configuration information, which allows items to be defined at different levels of the configuration hierarchy and cascaded down to the final collection of data. Second, if we are building a configuration section that handles something other than simple name-value pairs, we should provide a strong object model to represent the configuration section so that we achieve the goal of abstracting the XML representation of the configuration.

We will start by creating a simple class that implements the IConfigurationSectionHandler interface. This interface is required for all handlers and has a single Create method. This method takes in a parent configuration record, an HttpConfigurationContext, and an XmlNode object that represents the actual XML from the configuration file. It is expected to return an Object that represents this configuration information. In our case, we will be returning a NameValueCollection with the decrypted values from the configuration file.

The code for the configuration handler is shown in Listing 8-10. We'll focus on the configuration-specific issues and just briefly touch on the encryption mechanics.

Listing 8-10. Encrypted Configuration Section Handler

```csharp
using System;
using System.Configuration;
using System.Xml;
using System.Collections;
using System.Collections.Specialized;

namespace APress.ASPNetBestPractices
{
    /// <summary>
    /// Handles reading of encrypted configuration items and returning
    /// the decrypted values in a NameValueCollection.
    /// </summary>
    public class EncryptedConfigurationSectionHandler :
        System.Configuration.IConfigurationSectionHandler
    {

        public object Create(object parent, object configContext,
            System.Xml.XmlNode section)
        {
            NameValueCollection settings;
            NameValueCollection parentSettings;
            string key;
            string encryptedValue;
            string decryptedValue;
            XmlNodeList entries;
```

```
//If there is no parent, we need a new empty collection.
//But if there is, we need a new collection that includes the
//parent information.
if(parent == null)
    settings = new NameValueCollection();
else
{
    parentSettings = (NameValueCollection)parent;
    settings = new NameValueCollection(parentSettings);
}


try
{
    //get all of the items to be added
    entries = section.SelectNodes("//add");
    if(entries == null)
        throw new ConfigurationException(String.Format("The {0} section
            must have at least one \"add\" element in it.", section.Name),
            section);

    //Walk through the items and add each one to the collection,
    //decrypting as we go.
    for(int entryIndex = 0; entryIndex < entries.Count; entryIndex++)
    {
        //get the key and value from the element
        key =
            entries[entryIndex].Attributes.RemoveNamedItem("key").Value;
        encryptedValue =
            entries[entryIndex].Attributes.RemoveNamedItem("value").Value;

        //Just set this without worrying about the decryption
        //if there is no value.
        if(encryptedValue == "")
        {
            settings[key] = encryptedValue;
        }
        else
        {
            decryptedValue =
            APress.ASPNetBestPractices.ConfigurationSecurity.Decrypt
            (encryptedValue, true);
            settings[key] = decryptedValue;
        }
```

```
            }
        }
        catch(Exception ex)
        {
            throw new ConfigurationException("Error trying to process
configuration
                section", ex, section);
        }

        return settings;
    }
  }
}
```

We start out by checking for a parent section. If one exists, we use that for our container and simply add items to it based on their key values. This process works very well to support the cascading configuration and is made easier by our choice of a NameValueCollection for our objects. Next, we get all the "add" nodes from the configuration section and walk through them to get the values. We get the key and value attributes from the element and then decrypt the value if it is present. We add the decrypted value to the settings by using the key and, when we have processed all the nodes, we hand back the NameValueCollection to the caller.

As you can see, even a complex-sounding task like making an encrypted configuration section handler is extremely simple. Think of the power you get for the amount of work you have to put in, and it becomes clear that creating your own section handlers is definitely a best practice when the built-in handlers just don't do the trick.

You can find the code for the encryption and decryption functions in the code download for this chapter, available from the Apress Web site (http://www.apress.com). They use a simple method that uses machine-level key containers. To use the section, you first have to encrypt a value. We have created a Web page (that could easily be made a Web service) that will encrypt values for us to put in the configuration section. Figures 8-6, 8-7, and 8-8 show the value being encrypted, the value in the config file, and the resulting effect of requesting the configuration values from a page in our site.

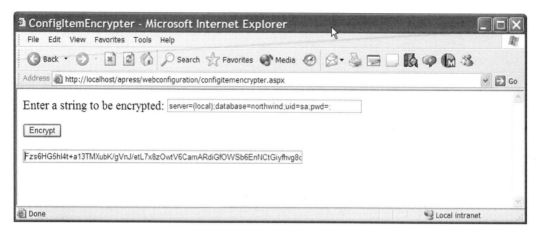

Figure 8-6. Encrypting the secret information

```
          </mailServers>
  -->
    <!-- End Example 4 -->
    <!-- Example 5
    NOTE: you will have to create a new encryted value on your machine for this to work.
    The values below will not work on a new machine because the key has not been installed.
  -->

                                        I

    <configSections>
        <section name="dbSettings" type="APress.ASPNetBestPractices.EncyptedConfigurationSectionHandler, P
    </configSections>
    <dbSettings>
        <add key="northwind" value="JReje1CbC/KOnLn1it0x+xaw21Va6kMv085MXVqan50y+DVlIpWSQqPkMyGBXgZtjmV01F
    </dbSettings>


    <!-- End Example 5 -->
    <!-- Standard Web configuration items -->
    <system.web>
        <compilation defaultLanguage="c#" debug="true" />
        <trace enabled="true" requestLimit="10" pageOutput="false" traceMode="SortByTime" localOnly="true'
        <sessionState mode="InProc" stateConnectionString="tcpip=127.0.0.1:42424" sqlConnectionString="dat
```

Figure 8-7. The encrypted information in the configuration file

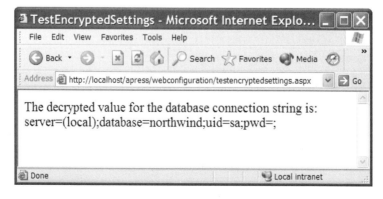

Figure 8-8. The decrypted value retrieved by the configuration section handler

Summary

As you know either from reading this chapter or from experience, the configuration system is very powerful, flexible, and extensible. You should take the time to understand every aspect of it before you decide to create your own configuration. Certainly there are limitations, but we have seen people create entire XML configuration systems because they did not realize that the ASP.NET configuration would cascade.

ASP.NET provides especially powerful features like those we have touched on in this chapter, including cascading web.config files, the ability to limit overrides of configuration with the location element and the allowDefinition attribute, and dynamically reloaded configuration. And, when the built-in tools do not meet your needs, you can take the sample section handler from Listing 8-10 as your template for creating your own section handler.

Index

A

activation, remoting, 162–63
Activator class, 171–72
Add method, Cache object, 29
allowDefinition attribute, 194–95, 196
allowOverride attribute, 193–95
Application Center Test
 data binding techniques, 131
 data grid control, 112
 data list control, 115
 output caching, 35–36
 partial-page caching, 139–40
 repeater control and list management controls, 118–19
 Session object, 44–49
 view state, 41–42
application domains
 appSettings section files and, 188
 caching and, 30
 configuration settings and, 30, 179, 189–91
 restarting, 30, 43
applications
 ASP.NET (see ASP.NET programming)
 configuring (see XML configuration system)
 dynamic reloading of configuration settings, 189–91
 losing cached information when restarting, 30
 Web service (see Web services)
 Windows service (see Windows Services)
appSettings element, 181, 185, 186–89
Apress Web site, 199
arrays
 IList interface and, 78
 JavaScript, 56–62
aspnet_client folder, 157–60
ASP.NET programming
 best practices (see best practices)
 client-side JavaScript (see JavaScript)
 code-behind model, 1–10 (see also code-behind model)
 configuring applications (see XML configuration system)
 data handling (see data handling)
 event wiring, 8–10 (see also events)
 inheritance in code behind, 5–8
 list management controls (see list management controls)
 remoting and Web services (see remoting; Web services)
 separating code from content, 3
 state management (see state management)
 user controls and server controls (see server controls; user controls)
aspx files. See Web pages
AsyncCallback mechanism, 169

asynchronous calls and remote communication, 168–69
attributes
 server control, 9, 53–54
 Web page, 32, 152
authentication and authorization, remote communication, 165
auto-formatting, turning off, 10
automatic reloading of configuration settings, 189–91

B

base class, code-behind inheritance, 5–8
best practices
 asynchronous calls and remote communications, 169
 avoiding unencrypted credentials in configuration files, 196
 built-in types for configuration settings, 184
 cascading configuration, 195
 checking for null configuration information, 184
 combining user controls with member method data binding, 135
 communicating between controls using events, 146–49
 content in .aspx files, 5
 creating XML files with DataSet objects, 25
 data list controls, 119
 DataView objects, 15
 dynamic user controls and server-side events, 152
 encapsulation of user controls, 144
 IIS as remoting host, 174
 IList interface, 78
 JavaScript in .js files or text files, 55, 65
 keeping less-dynamic and often-used data in caches, 23
 NameValueFileSectionHandler and default web.config settings, 188
 output caching, 36
 partial-page caching, 140
 reducing view state size, 37
 remoting and Web services, 164–69
 secure communications, 166
 server controls, 153–55
 server controls and user controls, 155–60
 setting cached data dependency with XML file, 27
 software design, 114
 SQL Server state management, 44
 static configuration information, 190
 strongly typed collections, 90
 templates, 152
 user controls, 143–52
 user interface code in code-behind files, 2

203